Siblings and the Family Business

A FAMILY
BUSINESS
PUBLICATION

Family Business Publications are the combined efforts of the Family Business Consulting Group and Palgrave Macmillan. These books provide useful information on a broad range of topics that concern the family business enterprise, including succession planning, communication, strategy and growth, family leadership, and more. The books are written by experts with combined experiences of over a century in the field of family enterprise and who have consulted with thousands of enterprising families the world over, giving the reader practical, effective, and time-tested insights to everyone involved in a family business.

FBCG, founded in 1994, is the leading business consultancy exclusively devoted to helping family enterprises prosper across generations.

FAMILY BUSINESS LEADERSHIP SERIES

This series of books is comprised of concise guides and thoughtful compendiums to the most pressing issues that anyone involved in a family firm may face. Each volume covers a different topic area and provides the answers to some of the most common and challenging questions.

Titles include:

All of the books were written by members of the Family Business Consulting Group and are based on both our experiences with thousands of client families as well as our empirical research at leading research universities the world over.

Siblings and the Family Business

Making It Work for Business, the Family, and the Future

Stephanie Brun de Pontet, Craig E. Aronoff,
Drew S. Mendoza, and John L. Ward

palgrave
macmillan

SIBLINGS AND THE FAMILY BUSINESS

Copyright © Family Business Consulting Group, 2012.

First published in 2012 by
PALGRAVE MACMILLAN®
in the United States—a division of St. Martin's Press LLC,
175 Fifth Avenue, New York, NY 10010.

Where this book is distributed in the UK, Europe and the rest of the world,
this is by Palgrave Macmillan, a division of Macmillan Publishers Limited,
registered in England, company number 785998, of Houndmills,
Basingstoke, Hampshire RG21 6XS.

Palgrave Macmillan is the global academic imprint of the above companies
and has companies and representatives throughout the world.

Palgrave® and Macmillan® are registered trademarks in the United States,
the United Kingdom, Europe and other countries.

ISBN: 978–0–230–34216–3

Library of Congress Cataloging-in-Publication Data is available from the
Library of Congress.

A catalogue record of the book is available from the British Library.

Design by Newgen Imaging Systems (P) Ltd., Chennai, India.

First edition: October 2012

10 9 8 7 6 5 4 3 2 1

Printed in the United States of America.

Contents

Exhibits

Introduction

Siblings and the Family Business

As he got himself ready to go into the office Andre knew he needed to keep his eagerness a little under wraps. His daughter Marie could read him like a book and he worried that if she knew how excited he was to have her start working full-time in the business, he would be unintentionally putting pressure on her, which his wife kept reminding him not to do.

The day members of the founding generation see their children taking an interest or having a voice in their enterprise is the day when the company officially becomes a family business. While the details differ for every family enterprise, few founders anticipate the challenges they will encounter translating their dream of passing on the business into reality. They may assume that passing the business on to their children is the most natural thing in the world, and while it is a common choice and can be done very successfully, there is nothing natural or automatic about the process. Rather, it requires a great deal of effort and planning on the part of all involved.

As families often have more than one child, the second generation typically includes more than one person, which leads to complexity that can provide both opportunities and challenges. The purpose of this book is to provide a roadmap to building an effective sibling team for your family's business. While the transition from the first to the second generation happens only once in the life of any given family business, as professional advisors in this field, we guide clients every day through these complexities. And while there are almost no solutions that fit all situations or formulas for success for every family business, our extensive experience accompanying clients on this journey gives us insight into the likely challenges you will encounter and enables us to offer wisdom based on research and knowledge gained in our work with thousands of family businesses in transition.

Teamwork is key to an effective, cohesive, fully functioning partnership in the sibling generation. Teamwork consists of a set of skills and attitudes that can be learned, and this book aims at helping the siblings in your family business attain those skills. Of course, siblings themselves cannot accomplish this in a vacuum. It takes the effort of all stakeholders to assure that siblings can become a team and work together successfully. Three groups in particular will play pivotal roles in the outcome: parents, in-laws, and the siblings themselves.

PARENTS OR FOUNDERS

If you are a founding generation parent, you are central to this process as you typically are in the position with the greatest authority. As the builder and owner of an enterprise, you have credibility and legal authority in your business. In addition, as head of the family you command moral authority in that system as well. While you are empowered to make decisions, your authority comes with responsibility, and the blurring of priorities between the needs of the family and the needs of the business can make it very hard for you to see a clear path forward to the next generation. While this book won't make the process easy, we hope to help you understand your sometimes seemingly conflicting feelings and goals so you can establish a plan that balances competing needs effectively.

IN-LAWS

If you are the spouse of a second-generation family member, you are in a tricky situation indeed. You may feel you are both loved and in some ways feared by your spouse's family—and this perception is often based in truth! Throughout this book we will show you how you and the members of the business-owning family can work toward a more harmonious, trusting relationship, one that not only supports your marriage but also supports the sibling team of which your spouse is a part.

SIBLINGS

If you are now or expect to become part of a sibling team leading a family business, your role is perhaps more challenging than you ever expected. How you and your siblings handle this responsibility is crucial to your success in both business and family. You have the responsibility of advancing the business, making it grow significantly for the benefit of your families and your children's families (rather than just the one family that it supported in your parents' generation). You must make a success of the business in your generation and set the stage for the generations that follow. What you do as a sibling team and how you do it will serve as the model for your children and will have consequences, good or bad, in their generation and the generations yet to come.

The transition of business leadership from the entrepreneurial founder to a family ownership team is a very vulnerable time in the life of a family business. Fully two-thirds of family firms will not survive beyond the first generation though they may outlast businesses not owned by a family (Ward 1987). With dedication, hard work, and expert guidance, the founding and sibling generation can work together to guide the business and family through this critical phase. The goal of this book is to help you do just that. It is full of wisdom, tips, guidelines, and the experiences gleaned from other families. We highlight situations for which you need to be prepared, point to the many tough decisions you will have to make, and offer some suggestions for building and maintaining a smoothly operating sibling team.

As you read, note that our bias is typically in favor of family ownership of businesses as good for business, employees, communities, and the owning families. This book is aimed at families where the second generation is involved and interested in the family's business. We assume that member of the second generation want to be more than passive bystanders and that they care about the business. It is our deeply held belief that a strong, healthy family enhances the possibility for a strong, healthy business, and vice versa. As such, our goal is to preserve the integrity of the family while serving the business, and the advice we present reflects these beliefs.

Ultimately, your challenge is to design creative solutions that best fit your family and its business. We will present excellent practices we have learned from our extensive visits with other sibling-led companies, such as methods for conflict management and decision making, a sibling code, and models for effective teamwork. We also encourage you to think outside the framework of just this book. The suggestions and ideas are meant to stimulate your thinking and conversations with your family to chart the best path forward. The transition to the sibling stage of family business ownership is an exciting journey, and we hope this book serves as a valuable tool to help guide you on your path.

Chapter 1

The Case for Sibling Partnerships

Planning for the continuity of your enterprise has never been more relevant. As the baby-boom generation (persons born between 1946 and 1964) is reaching and passing the age of 60, our culture is facing an unprecedented "bubble" of individuals moving toward retirement age. In an extensive survey of family businesses, wealth management advisors Laird Norton Tyee found close to 60 percent of family business owners were over 55 years of age, and 30 percent indicated they were 65 or older (Laird Norton Tyee 2007). Further, the *American Family Business Survey* found close to half of family business leaders planning to retire within the next ten years (American Family Business Survey 2007), suggesting the process of succession is now underway or around the corner for countless business families.

In addition to the unusual numbers of people approaching retirement—families in business may well have entered the "Age of Sibling Partnerships": we have seen a major shift over the past generation from transitioning the business typically to the firstborn son to a model where a founder more commonly transitions his or her enterprise to a team of siblings. Groups of siblings are increasingly involved in management, governance, and ownership of family enterprises. The performance of all of these groups is vastly improved by teamwork among them.

Among the many cultural norms driving this change are the following:

- *Young people are demonstrating more enthusiasm for the family business than ever before and, in our observation, are returning to the family firm in greater numbers.* This is particularly true when the family business is growing and successful—the next generation has grown up hearing about the challenges and the triumphs, and it is human nature to want to be a part of this winning team. Two additional trends may also be contributing to this change: a growing appreciation for the real and meaningful connection of family in a culture that is increasingly superficially connected and recent economic challenges that may make the family business an attractive career option when compared to corporate or professional alternatives. In fact, as family-owned enterprises tend to be less leveraged than other companies, many have weathered the economic crisis well and are continuing to grow and provide exciting career opportunities.

- *Parents are increasingly inclined to welcome all their children into the business as they seek to treat all their children as equals.* Firstborn sons are no longer presumptive successors. In the business families we work with, we are called upon less and less to help work out problems between an entrepreneurial father and a successor son and are asked more and more to help families in the development of a next-generation team as managers and/or owners.

- *As in the broader world of business, women are seeking more active roles in the management of their families' businesses and are more likely to be considered for top positions.* Whether as leaders or active owners, women are gaining a greater voice in family business. While we certainly have plenty of client examples of male-dominated industries where the women in the family are less involved in leadership, even in these families, women have increasingly taken on key functions in the sibling team through their active and engaged ownership role. Finding daughters assuming leadership positions in male-dominated industries is no longer unusual.

♦ *Ever-accelerating change means the knowledge of younger people is more valuable to their family businesses.* Wisdom that was applicable in the past is less likely to be applicable now or in the future. Founders recognize the contribution their sons and daughters can make in keeping a business on the cutting edge and may involve the next generation in important decisions earlier than ever. In addition, a team of siblings may approach issues from a variety of perspectives, creating a richer pool of ideas and stimulating creativity that can provide a competitive advantage in an increasingly turbulent and fast paced business world.

♦ *In many countries the laws that currently govern estate transfers support the formation of sibling teams.* Gifting stock rather than cash has tax advantages, in particular if this is done in small increments over time, taking advantage of dips in the value of the shares to gift more some years. Of course, if you (the founder) gift stock to all your children (as you want to treat them fairly and may not have many other equally valuable estate planning gifts to offer), in addition to reducing your estate taxes, you will have made your children business partners.

♦ *Greater awareness that many successful sibling partnerships exist makes others more willing to consider such partnerships.* While many business leaders may wonder if their own kids can get along well enough to be successful business partners, the great success of other families who have navigated this road provides families with the motivation to make the effort. A few examples of well-known family enterprises where a sibling leadership team has had success include Enterprise, Nordstrom, and Mars. As many sibling partnerships have yielded tremendous business success and profound family unity, these legacies serve as an inspiration to others.

Not only do these trends help to explain the growth in sibling partnerships, they also point to potential strengths that can come from this arrangement. For example, if the family is eager to continue with a family member at the helm, having a broader pool of candidates to consider (not just the firstborn and not just the males) will increase the odds that strong skills are available for fulfilling this responsibility. In addition, the ability to collaborate as a team of related owners, leaders, or directors can enrich decision making. The strengths of a sibling partnership obviously also come with related challenges, as you will see as you read on, however the sooner you think about how to develop the strongest possible team in your family, the better. Whether your family is considering a sibling partnership for the future, or perhaps brothers and sisters have already begun the difficult but rewarding process of team development, thoughtful deliberation, time spent working together, and a sense of farsightedness will provide tremendous benefits to your business and your family.

Chapter 2

Why This Transition Is So Hard

The Role of Complexity

The transition from the founding generation to the sibling generation is considered the most challenging of succession journeys for families in business for many reasons. Some significant ones include: the intensity of sibling relationships, the arrival of in-laws, and the difficulties the founder may have in letting go. We will touch on these and other challenges throughout this book. We start, however, with the overarching concept of complexity. Moving from one decider to needing to coordinate multiple decision makers for the business and the family is a fundamental change with a powerful impact. In addition, this complexity typically emerges in the context of important changes in the business (e.g., strategic, structural, technological, or financial evolution) and the family (e.g., aging parents slowing down) that increase the emotional intensity of every decision or change that must be considered in the process of transition.

GROWING COMPLEXITIES IN THE BUSINESS

It is common for the transition to a sibling partnership to happen in conjunction with (or just after) a period of significant growth in the business. The ownership transition occurs while the growing enterprise moves from being an entrepreneurial business run informally to one that needs more formal structures. What we frequently see is the business has grown past the point where it can be managed effectively with the systems that likely evolved to respond to the needs and preferences of the single decision maker, the founder. The required formalization is often referred to as the professionalization of the business. While this change is likely necessary, it often leads to much stress and anxiety throughout the organization, which creates a challenging context for the beginning of the sibling stage.

It is human nature to fear change, and it is not surprising that many employees, clients, vendors, and other stakeholders are anxious about what will happen when the founder leaves the business. As a result, there may be more resistance to further changes inside the organization, and some of the so-called old guard may worry that the arrival of more formal processes for decision-making, for example, is simply a sign that the soul of the business is being altered for the worse. While it is difficult to convince some people, if this institutionalization of what once might have been casual, intuitive processes is done right, it will support the success of a sibling partnership and position the company for further significant growth.

Some stakeholders may resist these changes, seeing them as a move toward bureaucracy. But in fact these additional structures are designed with the intention to position the company for growth and the family for harmony. Systems provide a framework for authority and accountability, and like decision making itself, these must be more deliberate and explicit when more than one owner is involved. While the formalization of decision-making processes can provide a vital framework to support the sibling team, it is important to remember that professionalization on its own is not a cure-all.

The significant changes concurrently happening in the business and family systems at the time of the generational transition can lead to an environment that feels like driving a car in a rainstorm. On a clear day, even a tricky road is manageable for a careful driver. However, in a storm with low visibility and slick roads, anxiety goes up, and the curves in the road are much harder to navigate. A business founder's departure (whether only under discussion, imminent, or sudden) is a significant event in the life of a business and can be experienced as a major storm by many stakeholders. Just thinking about a future change in leadership creates anxiety among key managers and can cause similar concerns among clients and suppliers. Even if the founder is considered a difficult manager or "behind the times," it is still human nature to fear change. The departure of the business founder, often an iconic figure revered by many and certainly a known and proven leader, is a big change that can lead to big fears.

In contrast, the siblings who are planning to take over are typically far less well known by the managers, customers, or suppliers of the business. Even those who have grown up in the business might still be pigeonholed as the boss's kid well into their thirties or forties. In fact, some customers or managers may have memories of these siblings fighting or showing up late to work when they were teenagers; and these old reputations can take a long time to overcome. While frustrating to many competent aspiring next-generation leaders, it always takes time to build strong professional bonds and a reputation for competence. Until that trust has been earned and the skill reliably demonstrated, the sibling generation will have to live with stakeholders who question its ability to successfully continue owning and leading the business. That is part of the challenging context in which the siblings must establish their partnership.

EMBRACING DIFFERENCES WHILE
BUILDING A TEAM

Not only must each member of the next generation demonstrate individual competence, but the siblings must also prove that they can operate as a unified team. In our experience, families with strong sibling teams have given a great deal of thought to how the siblings will work together. They have answered the following questions:

- Will one sibling be selected to lead the enterprise?
- Who will lead the family?
- Will several siblings collaborate to run the company?
- Will the siblings be primarily involved as owners while non-family executives lead the company?

While the correct leadership model will vary by family and industry (we will discuss sibling leadership models in chapter 7), the critical first step in continuity planning is to acknowledge that these questions must be answered and then to work through these choices together.

Through making these decisions and others, siblings need to come together as a team. Teams typically go through predictable stages of development referred to as forming, storming, norming, and performing (Tuckman 1965). As the stages imply, most teams stumble initially, so it is important not to get discouraged. Once siblings turn to the task of making decisions together (the forming stage), they may find themselves "storming" or getting to know one another in these new roles and engaging in heated arguments about work styles, goals, or priorities. Anger and tears at this stage may cause some families to wonder whether this is worth it. Despite the pain and difficulty, most families get through this stage to reach the norming stage when rules and agreements start being established and siblings begin to work together more effectively. With perseverance and patience, sibling teams reach the performing stage, functioning together like parts of a smoothly running, well-oiled machine, though one that will still need maintenance and occasional repair.

In addition to anticipating this normal developmental path to team building, recognize that the differences siblings bring to the table may cause conflicts but are actually a source of strength. Siblings differ in temperament (e.g., outgoing versus shy), knowledge, attitudes toward money (e.g., spendthrift versus saver), and in many other ways. Often it is because of growing up in the same household that they became so different, because children will naturally seek to find a niche in the family where they can belong (Bowen 1993). For example, not everyone can be the gregarious one; if your brother is funny, you may develop

EXHIBIT 2.1.   How to bring about creative solutions

Resolving conflicts requires patience and skill in any group. Here are some steps that siblings will find useful in establishing good norms as a team:

1. Define the problem first; don't start presenting a solution.
2. Prove understanding of the other person's concerns by restating them and asking if that understanding is correct.
3. Focus on debating the issue. Don't allow yourself to get personal. We believe in the saying: "Attack the problem; support the person."
4. If resolution comes slowly, brainstorm more alternatives. Ask others to propose new alternatives without initially evaluating any of them.
5. If the going gets tough, take a break. Come back to the topic the next day. In the meantime, resist dumping it on anyone else.
6. Words and behavior used while addressing a problem will long be remembered. To gain perspective, one family we know pretends that the discussion is being videotaped for viewing by the next generation.

a different style to stand out. Perhaps Art is visual, and Kelly is more verbal. Kent may be extroverted and Anne very analytical. As a result, not only do you have more than one voice to manage in a sibling partnership, these can be very different voices indeed!

While differences can make it harder to understand one another, they should be valued because they introduce a variety of talents, perspectives, and ideas essential to success in a sibling partnership. The complexity that emerges in a second-generation family and company require a range of skills, including sophisticated business know-how, deep emotional intelligence, and a great capacity to bring family members together. A diverse sibling team is more likely to combine a range of abilities and can therefore provide stronger leadership. For example, a sibling pair where one is highly oriented to sales and the other to operations may do better than a sibling pair where both are focused on sales. Likewise, while the sibling team that is entirely focused on cautious growth may agree more quickly on strategy, a sibling team with a balance of aggressive and cautious temperaments may strike the right balance of reaching for opportunities without taking excessive risks. It is also worth noting that in our experience working with sibling teams all over the world, we find sibling partnerships with gender diversity have more harmony and better results than those that are either all male or all female; this supports the concept that differences enrich the team overall. The point is that siblings should seek to understand one another's views and celebrate their differences even as they need to overcome them daily to reach decisions.

While the diversity of a sibling team is a source of strength, siblings must understand and acknowledge that they hear, think, decide, and

---

EXHIBIT 2.2.   **Complicating factors for sibling partnerships**

- Varying styles of decision making: fast versus deliberate, high-risk versus low-risk ...
- Differences in communication styles
- Varying degrees of commitment and interest in the business
- Unproven business leadership and uncertainty regarding ownership team
- Presence of owners who do not work in the business (knowledge gap)
- Different expectations around allocation of profit (growth versus dividends)
- Presence of spouses (didn't grow up with business or in this family)
- Need to provide financial independence to G1 and effects on business and G2

communicate differently. They need to develop skills to deal with their differences, such as communication skills, listening skills, empathy, and appreciation for differences. They must accept their differences and seek shared priorities and interests. With everyone's commitment and the right structures, systems, and procedures in place, conflict can be managed effectively, and differences can benefit the company and the family. In fact, the most important common thread we see in well-functioning sibling teams is a set of shared core values and a deep respect for one another, including for all differences (see chapter 6 for a discussion of clarifying shared values).

Making Decisions as a Sibling Team

Whether siblings work in the business or primarily collaborate as owners, siblings will need to make decisions together, and their decision-making process will likely be quite different than the first generation's approach. In the founding generation, one person typically makes almost all key decisions: he or she owns the company so is legally empowered to make decisions and actively leads the company so employees expect her or him to make decisions. If the company grows substantially, there may be other important decision makers or advisors who provide input, but most commonly, the proverbial buck stops with the owner-manager. By contrast, when it comes time for the next generation to make key decisions, the siblings will have to consult with one another and work as a team to decide on many matters. Even if one of the siblings is the designated leader of the business, that person will at times need input from the other siblings on matters of ownership or on issues affecting the intersection of family and business. While getting the perspective of more than one person may well enrich the decision that is reached, decision making by a team is slower and more complicated than when one owner makes decisions on his or her own.

Yannik Industries has experienced significant growth since the founder retired five years ago, in part thanks to the strong skills of the second-generation leaders who have expanded their father's business into important new markets. Four siblings share ownership equally and are trying to decide on appropriate dividend levels. The two siblings who work in leadership roles in the business see value in lower dividends in order to reinvest more in operations. One sibling who works part-time in the business is seeking more income from dividends to help him cover the expenses of his passion for sailing. The last sibling is not working in the business and not that engaged in the issues but has expressed concern that it doesn't seem "fair" that the younger brother earns so much less money than the two in leadership.

As we can see in the case of Yannik Industries, one challenge siblings face is balancing competing needs and priorities. While all businesses must consider the trade-off between reinvesting in the company or providing income to shareholders, different siblings may view this trade-off differently and thus add still more complexity to this choice. Some siblings may be averse to risk and eager to harvest some profits or diversify their holdings. Others may want to reinvest all profit in the business and have the business take on debt in pursuit of growth. In addition, some siblings may confuse business issues with notions of family fairness, blurring the intersection of business and family and causing emotionally intense disagreements. These tensions between the siblings may be compounded by competing demands for money to support business growth and a desire to buy out the first generation to allow the parents to be fully independent from the business and to enjoy the financial freedom they worked so hard to build.

In addition, this example illustrates another common challenge to the decision-making process of sibling teams: different levels of knowledge about the company or even business in general. While all members of some sibling teams may be full-time leaders in the family business, many sibling teams include shareholders who are not employed in their family's business. Unless shareholders not working in the business make a conscious effort to stay current, uneven levels of knowledge or interest can result. At the same time, siblings who work in the business should make every effort to inform their siblings about the company, helping to keep them abreast of important issues or opportunities and to feel fully connected to their shared asset.

In order to manage these competing demands (and countless others), sibling teams typically need more processes and structures than did their parents. For example, siblings may need to have monthly or quarterly ownership meetings to make certain decisions as a group. Further, sibling teams need clear policies to guide them in making difficult decisions; for example, are all decisions taken by consensus or will the majority rule in some cases? And what happens if a sibling wants to sell his or her shares? Taking the time to consider how the group will handle difficult situations before they arise is prudent planning. Siblings may also need additional financial reports to be regularly created to promote communication with owners not working in the company. Even for family matters more structure and planned meetings may be needed, as there is no longer a single kitchen table around which all gather.

If you consider how many changes must occur at the same time to respond to the growing complexity of the business and the family at the sibling stage, it is not surprising that this is considered the most challenging of generational transitions.

Chapter 3

Challenges and Opportunities Facing the Siblings

The sibling partnership stage is generally more intense and volatile than any other. As a result of their growing up together, the level of intimacy is higher among siblings than it is in the cousin generation that follows. This deeper knowledge of one another can foster a particularly strong partnership between individuals who can finish each other's sentences, share each other's passion, knowledge, and commitment to the business, and care for one another as only siblings can. On the other hand, some siblings really know how to get under each other's skin, have a harmful shared history that leads to mistrust, or are simply constantly in competition for the attention and favors of their parents. Whether the family history is good or bad, it will have profoundly shaped each individual and the dynamics between them, making the emotional tenor of the family business particularly intense for siblings.

GROWING UP WITH THE BUSINESS

One element of the shared history between siblings is that they will have a direct relationship to the business because they all grew up with the company taking up a lot of the energy and time of the family.

Siblings will often hear about what is going on at the company at the kitchen table, and as the first generation likely has to work long hours, they may at times pull all members of their direct family into the business to pitch in on small tasks during the busy season or to participate in key celebrations. Many children of business founders will have their first summer job experience helping out at the shop or around the office. What is interesting is that each individual will react differently to this experience, even in the same family.

Some siblings develop a real passion and interest for business that is enhanced by their early acquisition of relevant knowledge and experience, and this will likely make their desire to be involved with the business that much stronger. Others will resent the business, almost developing jealousy toward this entity that is often treated as the "favorite child" in the family. Siblings who grow up resenting the degree to which the business rules the family are unlikely to want to work in the business, and they may even have trouble committing effectively to an engaged ownership role as adults. As a result, some sibling teams may not include all siblings. Careful estate planning or finding ways to allow a family member to sell his or her stock to the business or to other siblings can help deal with such issues. While these may be uncomfortable and at times challenging situations to address, they cannot be ignored. Building an effective sibling ownership or management team is challenging enough among siblings who actually want to be a part of the process.

EMOTIONAL ISSUES

Consider two brothers, Ivan and Arthur. Ivan is 39, eight years older than Arthur. Ivan views himself as responsible and sees Arthur as somewhat irresponsible and just living off the fat of the family business. Arthur, after all, was the baby of the family. For the first eight years of his life, Ivan had been the center of attention and praise. Then Arthur came along, and Ivan had to fend for himself while little Arthur had everything taken care of for him.

> *To this day, Ivan treats his younger brother like a baby, and Arthur reacts like one. To make matters worse, their parents, seeing that the brothers aren't working well together in the business, intervene and make decisions their sons should be making or hold on to responsibilities their sons should be assuming.*

As this example illustrates, emotional issues frequently get in the way of a sibling partnership's success. Working out the issues of family relationships and family history is essential for keeping these from getting in the way of rational decision making. If parents haven't helped their children develop the skills for team success, the siblings, as adults, must develop those skills—including communications, conflict resolution, and shared decision making—on their own.

A number of emotional factors unique to brothers and sisters can affect how they work together as a team. Understanding these and realizing that every sibling partnership is affected by most of these issues will help you be more objective, more knowledgeable, and even more compassionate in dealing with them. This increased awareness will empower you as a group. Some common emotional issues that often affect siblings in family business are discussed below.

The controlling behavior of entrepreneurial parents. Many business founders are high controllers. That is, combining an entrepreneur's tendency toward control with normal parental feelings can produce parents who want to govern the attitudes, the values, the opinions, the dress—in short, the overall behavior—of offspring, not just during childhood but throughout life. The business itself can feed the need to control. For example, a business-owning family can be highly visible in the community, giving parents concern about how what their children do might reflect on the business. Some parents even use the business to control their children, either through rewards or punishments: "You will rearrange your vacation to come to the family meeting or else!" While you cannot control how your parents behave, you *can* manage your response to these behaviors. Simply being aware that this dynamic may be present in your family can help you think of how it may influence your (and your siblings) feelings and behaviors.

The controlling nature of entrepreneurs leads many to continue to make all significant decisions, even after their children and others have proven their competence. The problem is that this will negatively impact the development of the sibling team, because, in this situation, siblings do not get sufficient practice in making decisions together. Further, many parents (often with the best of intentions) tend to suppress conflict in the family instead of using it to encourage the development of communication skills. Communication skills are critical for members of the next generation to resolve the disagreements they will inevitably face.

Sibling rivalry. While a certain amount of competition for the time and attention of parents is normal in any sibling relationship, adult siblings need to be aware of the rivalries between them and take steps to resolve these. As adults trying to work as a unit in business, members of the next generation need to see each other in new ways; they may even have to get to know each other all over again. Each sibling must consciously strive for less dependence on parental approval to minimize the rivalry felt toward brothers and sisters. One way to make this happen is to make the siblings' approval become more important than parents' approval.

Adopting your parents' baby (that they struggle to give up). It is often said that a business is the parents' other child or even favorite child. They created it, just as they created their human children, and their feelings for it are profound, just as their feelings for their children are profound. As the sibling team must be established concurrently with the founders' struggle of letting go, the emotional stress of each will affect the others. For example, the entrepreneur's need to continue to feel relevant in the business he or she founded may slow the process of passing on authority to the next generation. Similarly, some siblings may feel ambivalence about their growing authority at the company if they feel this is playing a role in the difficulties their father is facing regarding retirement.

The age spread of siblings. Older siblings are typically the first to enter the business and get a head start on their younger siblings.

An individual with a running start may have a big advantage in a situation where the family is looking to find the definitive leader for the business or if the parents are ready to retire before the younger siblings have had a chance to prove themselves. For example, if the age spread is eight years, there could be one child in their midthirties with a lot of experience and another who is just starting in the company after graduate school. If the parents are looking to retire soon, they may be inclined to put more effort into training the eldest, who will be ready sooner. On the other hand, some parents may favor the younger sibling in this situation because "they love their children equally" and want to give a boost to the baby of the family. Not surprisingly, if the age spread is contributing to any kind of favoritism, this will certainly feed into sibling rivalry and its negative effects.

Mother's tendency to want to "save the family." Often a mother's desire to preserve the family is so strong that she may become involved to the point of manipulating or moderating any news that she picks up about disagreements or disputes in the business. Siblings need to be aware of this pattern and address it with sensitivity. One significant consequence of this desire is that it sends the message that conflict is dangerous; thus, it may lead the family to suppress important disagreements rather than learn the necessary skills to work through issues to acceptable solutions.

Successful sibling teams tend to be those who also work at getting to know one another as individuals. Siblings sometimes believe they know one another better than they actually do. Since you grew up in the same house and have many shared memories, it is easy to assume you know everything there is to know about one another. As individuals leave home, go off to college or jobs, and otherwise develop as adults, they change and evolve. The truth is sometimes family members are slow to recognize these changes, and this can lead to misunderstanding and frustration. It is very important for sibling teams to spend time together away from the business. Meeting every week or two or on semi-business occasions, without spouses, helps siblings increase their comfort with each other and enhance their ability to communicate effectively.

BENEFITS OF BLOOD TIES

It can be easy to dwell on the emotional hurdles facing siblings and feel convinced that this must always be a bad arrangement, but we find many siblings make powerful and effective teams. Usually raised together, siblings often share values, and this should make for more effective joint decision making. Shared values are an essential basis for any meaningful collaboration. While growing up with the founder does come with some of the challenges mentioned above, the sibling generation has the benefit of very intimate knowledge of the business because it was part of conversations around the kitchen table and of many other aspects of their childhood experience. In addition, assuming that the presence of the business in the family system did not lead to a lot of resentment, the siblings may have grown up with a sense of loyalty and psychological attachment to the enterprise and deep pride in the family's legacy related to the business. This shared passion and caring for the company often helps siblings to see the big picture and accept certain decisions or compromises because they appreciate how they benefit the greater good, even if a particular choice would not be their preference.

Finally, all siblings grow up fighting and negotiating with one another, and though at times unpleasant, if this is allowed to take its natural course, it will give them far more practice in working together and finding solutions than unrelated business partners would have. Through these experiences, good and bad, growing up as family leads to bonds of love and trust that can create a foundation for deep and powerful collaboration, often setting up a positive relationship between the work of the business and family connectivity. Certainly understanding these emotional issues enables members of the sibling group to become better prepared to compensate for weaknesses and build on the strengths that will help them collaborate effectively.

FOUR KEY TASKS OF THE SIBLING STAGE

In addition to understanding their shared history, siblings must accomplish four core tasks in the transition from the founding generation. It can take time and effort, but sibling partnerships can develop very effective leadership of their enterprise and stronger personal bonds in the family through their collaboration on these tasks:

1. *Become an autonomous, independent team.* This means the siblings must become independent of their parents. And while parents will talk about how much they want this to happen, unconsciously they may not always be ready for this change and may do many things that get in the way of this independence. In the natural and almost inevitable tug-of-war in which the siblings test their autonomy and the parents assert their power, the siblings must take responsibility for doing what they can to make the transition a reality (and not wait for the parents to initiate and conduct the changeover). One powerful step you can take as siblings to become a team is to clarify your shared purpose. Work together to answer the question of why you are in business together. It is valuable to think about what you are hoping to accomplish and to clarify and articulate your shared guiding principles: what will unite you as a team?

2. *Take the initiative as successors.* The more the siblings take responsibility for and control of developing themselves individually and as a team and the more they seize the initiative, the more likely the succession will proceed in a timely way and be successful. True, occasionally a patriarch will see sibling interaction as a plot or conspiracy to get rid of him, but that doesn't happen often. In addition, while the parent generation may be preventing you from asserting your authority in some areas of the business, you can still take the initiative to work as a team on identifying opportunities to add value and determine how you will make decisions together. Find a project where you can practice making decisions and working as a team. An excuse we

often see the senior generation offer for not letting go is that the kids don't get along; thus, if you actively demonstrate this not to be true, you build your credibility in addition to teamwork skills.

3. *Put structure and strategies into place that will help the business grow significantly.* In addition to the changes you will need to institute in how decisions are made in an enterprise with a more complex ownership group, the business needs to grow to sustain this ownership model as well. You have been raised in a family that probably had a good standard of living. But the business needed to support only one set of parents and children when you were young. Now, you all want your own family to live at least as well as you did growing up. For that to happen, the business has to grow sufficiently to support all siblings and their families; you cannot just sit on the laurels of what was built in the past.

4. *Position the next generation for success.* The job is not done until the stage is properly set for handing the business to your own children. This means putting into place policies, procedures, and structures that will support the success of the next generation of family business owners and leaders.

EXHIBIT 3.1.   **Goals for sibling teams**

- Take charge of succession. Stop waiting for your parents' permission.
- Overcome sibling rivalry.
- Convince parents that there won't be a family rupture once they leave the business. (Otherwise, they won't leave.)
- Communicate with your parents and with non-family executives as a unit.
- Communicate openly with one another.
- Get to know one another again as adults; invest in your personal relationships with one another.

- Become an autonomous, independent unit.
- Demonstrate your ability to work together.
- Develop your competence and skills.
- Put structures and strategies in place that will help the business grow significantly in your generation.
- Position the next generation for success.

Chapter 4

Setting the Stage

The Role of the Founding Generation

FOUNDERS: CONTROLLING
AND LARGER THAN LIFE

Some of the strong personality characteristics that enable entrepreneurs to succeed against the odds in launching their business may actually complicate the transition to the sibling generation. For example, children who are raised by controlling parents may not develop great self-confidence which could affect their ability to build a team or to make decisions on their own, (Deci and Ryan 1985) weaknesses that could affect their eventual sibling partnership. In addition, the effort of launching a business means a founder must often be away from home. These frequent absences can lead to particularly intense sibling rivalry as children compete for the parent's very limited attention. In some families this intense rivalry leads siblings to grow distant from and even mistrustful of one another, adversely affecting their ability to collaborate as business partners. Sadly, some entrepreneur-parents like to foster competition among their children because they believe it will "toughen them up."

Business leadership is also affected by a business founder's controlling style. Founders often develop a hub-and-spoke style of management where they are at the center and all decisions go through them. Consequently, other managers in the business, including their children, may not develop strong decision-making skills or experience in being accountable for the results of their decisions. This very centralized style of leadership typically becomes increasingly inefficient as the company's size and complexity increase.

Many business builders cast a giant shadow because it is hard for anyone to top all they have accomplished. The more the first generation has accomplished in business, the more overwhelming this may feel to the next generation trying to fill those shoes. Frustrations the founder's heirs may harbor from their childhood may also be colored by the founder's legacy or his or her larger-than-life presence. While no one wants to begrudge the entrepreneur his or her accolades, this earned respect can sometimes make it exceptionally hard for members of the next generation to craft their own vision or make needed changes in the business. The reality is that businesses and markets change and evolve over time, and even the most enlightened leader's vision needs to be reviewed at least once every generation.

In terms of management, the structures that worked for the lone, entrepreneurial founder may not work at the sibling stage. If the members of the successor generation are to function effectively as co-owners and/or fellow employees, they must adopt procedures and practices far different from the ones that were successful for the founder. However, the respect all have for the founder may hamper them in making these needed changes. Any innovation initiated by the next generation may meet with resistance from stakeholders who see changes as indications of disloyalty to the founder.

Though the founding generation does not hold *all* the cards to the success of the sibling team, parents or founders should consider a number of tasks or priorities (well in advance of transition) to give siblings the best chance at success. These tasks, which we will further detail throughout this chapter, include the following:

♦ raising your children in ways that encourage their working together as an independent unit;

- adopting personal behavior toward each other as a couple, toward your children, and toward their spouses that supports a sibling partnership;
- putting policies and practices into place that will provide a foundation for the partnership and encouraging the sibling team's efforts to continue that process;
- preparing for your exit from the business.

PREPARING THE KIDS

Many founders worry that if their children don't get along as kids, they will not be able to own or run a business together as adults. While some siblings are "wired" so differently or develop such poor relationships with one another that it will prevent them from being effective business partners, most siblings have the capacity and spirit to collaborate. When children are very young, and as they become teenagers and young adults, much can be done to nourish their ability to work together and to channel sibling rivalry into constructive pursuits.

It is important that parents act as though their business will evolve into a sibling partnership at some point in the future. At the very least, this means not telling an oldest child, "This business will be all yours someday." That statement may very well come back to haunt you as a parent if other children demonstrate more business ability and interest. To prepare them for a future partnership, brothers and sisters as early as their preteen years can be given tasks to do together that have consequences. For example, consider these assignments, which are appropriate for siblings from ages 8 to 18:

- Give them $500 as a group (or $2,000 or $5,000). Tell them you want them to figure out what stocks to invest the money in. Ask them to come up with a plan for learning about the stock market together and agreeing on what stocks to buy.

◆ Ask the kids to decide together by a specified date where the family will go on its next vacation. Tell them that they must agree.
   The older they are, the more details they can decide. Observe
   how well they share the responsibility and participation.

In one family we worked with, the children were responsible for allo-
cating the family foundation budget for some education-related projects. They attended foundation board meetings as of their thirteenth
birthday. They had to work as a committee to determine which education grant requests would get funded and present their reasoning to
the board. In another family, which had a summer home on a lake, the
children's love of waterskiing became the focal point of team building
at an early age. They had to take turns, with one sibling skiing, another
operating the boat, and still another spotting the skier. They had to
learn to cooperate with one another, to look after each other's safety
and welfare, and to manage the cost of fuel for the boat and keep the
boat in good repair.

As a parent, when you give children tasks of this nature, you help
them build skills for success as a team: communications, conflict resolution, and shared decision making. It may not be easy, but parents must
resist the temptation to step in with a solution. When parents step in, the
children are deprived of the opportunity to work things out themselves,
as a unit. We recommend, instead, an "oversight" approach and letting
the kids work things out with parents refereeing only enough to make
sure that nobody gets hurt.

The same strategy can be used when the children grow up and
begin working in the business. Give your children meaningful tasks
that have serious consequences and expect them to come up with
solutions. While it will be harder to find the appropriate task, find
projects for your adult children to tackle together even if they are not
all working in the business. They will likely still need to learn to work
together on family matters and potentially as eventual owners with
fewer natural opportunities to develop the important relationship and
collaboration skills they will need. Beyond the benefit of learning to

work together, these opportunities may help ensure that your children who are not working in the business stay adequately informed and connected to the enterprise. The challenge will be to find a project oriented to the ownership role where young adults can take the lead and accommodating the scheduling and geographic constraints if some of your children have growing professional roles that have moved them out of state.

Keep challenging your children with tasks they must accomplish as a unit. While it is also important for each child to be given independent responsibilities, you can only foster a team when they are required to undertake tasks together to develop their working relationships. Some parents shy away from assigning projects for their children to accomplish together in an effort to avoid conflict and confrontation among them. Siblings will have some confrontations as they learn to work together, but it is far better that they get in the habit of working through their differences and learn that conflict is not dangerous. Thanks to this experience, when the siblings must resolve tough issues later on, they will have developed the skills to work things out together.

We also recommend that parents expose their children to other leadership models. Encourage them to visit successful businesses where leadership is structured differently than it is at your company and to share with the family what they learned. Invite representatives from other family businesses that have sibling teams collaborating in management as well as from businesses where the siblings share ownership responsibility but have one designated enterprise leader to your family meetings. Ask them to talk about how their systems work, about what works well, and about what doesn't work so well.

Finally, when the members of the next generation are in their thirties, we often advise parents to assign them the project of articulating their plan for the enterprise. While this is a complex assignment, if the siblings have practiced working together and developed knowledge of the enterprise, each other, and the ownership role, they are ready for the challenge (often with the help of a professional experienced in

EXHIBIT 4.1.   Ten tips for founders

1. Assume that your business may evolve into a sibling partnership. Avoid saying to any one of your children, "Someday this business will be all yours."

2. From the time your children are young, promote the partnership skills of listening, communicating, resolving conflict, and working together.

3. Recognize that what works in the founder's stage of the business often will not work at the sibling stage. Understand that your children will likely have to reinvent the company.

4. Before they're needed, put policies and procedures in place that will support the sibling partnership.

5. Introduce the concept of prenuptial agreements early— before the kids have serious boyfriends and girlfriends.

6. Welcome in-laws and educate them about the business. If you want them to care and behave like family, you have to treat them as family.

7. Treat the sibling team as a unit. Do not try to divide and conquer. Do not create aggressive competition between them.

8. Let leadership among the siblings emerge. At the sibling stage there may be a need for more than one leader and for different styles of leadership.

9. Be patient; do not always step in when things are not going smoothly.

10. Plan how you will spend your time and direct your energy once you relinquish control of the day-to-day leadership of the business and implement the plan.

facilitating this process). The directive might go something like this: "Come up with your plan for the future of the business. Make sure the plan speaks for all of you. Then bring it to us, and we'll work through it together before putting it in motion." In this way the challenge is in the siblings' hands. By figuring out a way of getting over their rivalries or using their rivalries to advantage and by demonstrating their knowledge and ability, they can earn leadership and control of the business.

THE IMPACT OF FAMILY RELATIONSHIPS

The actions of parents provide powerful examples and valuable lessons for the next generation's lives. Because they have grown up together, the impact of this modeling on the business partnership between siblings in a family business is more intense than it might be for other business partners who are not family members or relatives. Founding parents model much regarding partnership through their marriage. Marriage represents the family partnership—roles and responsibilities of each partner may differ, but there needs to be a smooth and respectful collaboration between husband and wife to make the family work well. While every couple has disagreements, it is helpful to acknowledge differences as a couple and not let the disagreement be lived out through the children. Unfortunately, in some families where the parents are in discord, one child may affiliate with the father and another with the mother; this plants the seeds for additional tension between the children later on, and the parents model ineffective conflict resolution if they encourage this. Parents should make it clear to the younger generation that the parents' problems as a couple are the parents' problems, not the children's.

Families also need to avoid "triangulation": where one party to a conflict or disagreement brings a third party into the situation rather than addressing the problem directly with the source of his or her frustration or concern. It is very common for siblings to take up an issue they have with one another with their parents because they learned to do this from an early age. For example, if Ali today feels Kristen is undermining his authority in the marketing department, he needs to take that up with Kristen directly and not involve their parents. Of course, parents can sometimes triangulate their kids. For example, if all the siblings are working in the business and Mark, the youngest, is consistently late for work, his mother may express her displeasure not to Mark but to his sister, Suzanne. In this instance, Mom should talk to Mark about his tardiness and leave Suzanne out of it. When parents triangulate, we advise their offspring not to permit it. In this case, Suzanne could say, "Mom, that's something you should take up with Mark."

It is also important that children grow up feeling valued and appreciated for the talents and skills they have. Unfortunately, some parents feed into unhealthy rivalry between their children by constantly comparing one to the other, in sports, in school, and eventually in the business. For example, if one child has greater academic success, it does not help to constantly point that out to the other siblings, and asking why they can't do as well in math will *not* motivate them to study harder. Indeed, it may well have a negative impact on their self-image and relations with one another! While we all want our children to try hard and succeed, some will do better than others in any given area. In our experience, the strongest sibling teams are made up of individuals with different capabilities but with uniform respect for one another and for what each brings to the table.

Another area where parents must monitor their behavior is in their treatment of their children's spouses. In-laws are so important to the success of a sibling partnership that we have devoted a whole section to the topic (see chapter 5). Parents can do much to set the tone for acceptance of in-laws as partners, welcome them into the family, and teach them about the business. Giving conscious thought as a family to the role of spouses in the family business is a good thing. When parents and siblings can reach a consensus about the role of the in-laws, the involvement of those who married into the family becomes a matter of policy rather than personalities; in other words, spouses aren't excluded just because someone in the family doesn't like a brother's wife.

POLICIES AND PRACTICES

Parents go a long way toward setting their children up for success when they, as founders, begin to establish procedures and practices that will serve the next generation well. By initiating family meetings in the first generation of a family business, you can set a precedent for open communication and shared decision making. Thus, when your daughter becomes the CEO in your children's generation, she will already have learned the value of communicating with her brothers and sisters and sharing business information with them. She will also have a platform for doing so.

Other valuable systems that far-sighted founders may establish in the first generation include an outside board; that is, a board with independent directors (ideally business peers) in addition to key family members. Founders who are mindful of the challenges that come with the overlap of family and business may also have begun to devise some formal policies for the business, such as a code of conduct for the family or guidelines for the employment of family members.

Most founders have neither a board of directors nor written policies. The responsibility to establish the practices and policies that will enable the business to grow, thrive, and survive for the future often falls on the next generation. Some founders may be uncomfortable with the changes this brings to how decisions are made in the business. Yet, keep in mind that whenever the members of the next generation develop a policy or establish a procedure, they are gaining strength and experience in working as a team. Remember, too, that in seeking family and business growth in the face of increasing complexity, the sibling team will need to transform an entrepreneurial, informal organization to one governed and managed by more formalized, institutionalized policies, procedures, and systems. Finally, recognize that the second generation is working to prepare the family and the business for an eventual third generation of leadership, thus sustaining the entrepreneur's legacy. (For more information on governance structures and policies for family business, please see our books in this series, listed on

p. ii: *Family Business Governance: Maximizing Family and Business Potential* and *Developing Family Business Policies: Your Guide to the Future.*)

EXIT PLANNING

No business owner's job is done until she or he has planned to exit. This means planning for family and business leadership succession and also developing an active plan for your life after your business leadership. These plans ensure that the future holds promise for the entrepreneur personally as well as for the business and his or her kids.

Most business owners love their work, and many don't want to let go. They haven't considered what they would do in retirement. This lack of a personal plan can derail the best-laid business succession plans. Research on retirement finds the centrality of a job to a person's identity is inversely associated with the expectations that person has for retirement (Gee and Baillie 1999) and with the timing of retirement (Elder and Pavalko 1993). While the sibling team needs to be patient and develop empathy for how hard this process is for their parent, the founder needs to take responsibility for crafting a viable exit plan and sticking to it.

> *Upon becoming CEO in his midfifties, one son who had experienced years of brutal power struggles with his father turned to his board and announced that he would retire at age 62. He told the members of the next generation to figure out the next transition and get ready; he would help and provide resources in the form of consultants. "If my dad had said that to me at any time," he said, "that would have been the greatest thing he could have done for me." In effect, this CEO told the next generation: "It is my job to make this your job."*

While it is true that the emotional issues in succession are harder to navigate, money is hardly an irrelevant variable to this planning. The study by Laird Norton Tyee mentioned earlier found that the family business is the primary source of income for well over 90 percent of families owning businesses. This suggests that the retiring founders will likely remain economically dependent on the success of the company unless they have established a mechanism to assure their financial independence from the business. Ideally, exit planning includes providing for financial transitions in the family business through appropriate estate planning. However, the study by Kennesaw State University cited earlier found 86 percent of family business owners in the United States had not done any estate planning beyond a basic will. Moreover, 70 percent of all those surveyed could not estimate their estate-tax liabilities, and 43 percent could not estimate their business's market value. These are alarming statistics because lack of appropriate tax planning has lead to the forced sale of many successful family enterprises and may preclude your next generation from even having an opportunity to work together as a team.

THE IDEAL

Ideally, what will happen is this: the parents will follow the practices and suggestions outlined above, encouraging and developing the team-building skills of their children, when they are very young and also later when they are young adults in the business. If the groundwork has been well established in this manner, the sibling team can be put into a trial leadership role, as in a "family-in-the-business committee" with increasing management responsibilities and/or taking over the responsibilities of ownership decisions before they legally become owners. In effect, the parents and the partnership of siblings develop a joint venture that will last for a period of time. The parents say to the siblings: "In addition to your regular jobs, you are responsible for planning the future of the company." The parent CEO remains the chief executive, in charge of strategic decisions, but the next generation will increasingly be responsible for planning and initiating change.

This process allows the parents to see how well the siblings work together. It also reveals how much they *want* to work together, which may ultimately decide whether they are in fact going to be a sibling partnership for the long term. The process also enables the sibling team to begin to develop its own leadership and decision-making systems.

What this process requires of parents is patience and self-control. It is important that parents *not* step in and take command when things aren't going smoothly, for example, when differences surface among siblings and the team becomes paralyzed, when decisions are made only slowly or not at all, or when a poor decision is made. Parents have to be willing to accept some negative business consequences as a cost of learning and going forward. The founding parent also may need patience because his or her controlling nature may lead him or her to see the indecision and the time the team process takes as signs of weakness. Entrepreneurs pride themselves on being decisive and reporting to nobody. A sibling team collaboration goes against this style.

As bumpy as it can sometimes be, the process of the siblings learning to work together through a "family-in-the-business" committee is a great way for them to develop and work on their partnership. Over time, several years perhaps, the solution to future leadership in the sibling generation may well emerge from this process. Sometimes a consultant can be invaluable here, for example, coaching the siblings to make better decisions or helping them to manage conflict and use it constructively. Ideally, with the help of the board, the siblings begin to see for themselves the challenges and potential of the business and who can best handle the leadership responsibility.

An alternative to this ideal occurs when it becomes apparent to the parents that there is one proper leader, and they decide sooner rather than later, such as when their son is 32, not when he's 52,who the next CEO will be. Such a decision may be made because the son is so clearly able, or because he is able and ready while his siblings are still very young and their abilities have not yet emerged. The parents find themselves in a position of having to make a choice, and they do so lovingly, expressing their appreciation for the other children and including them as part of the ownership team. The process of transition to one son as CEO may take five years or more to complete. Meanwhile, his siblings have an opportunity to adapt to the decision and to decide whether or not they wish to commit themselves to the company with that brother at the helm, get another job, or go to graduate school and move on with their lives.

What is important to remember in this model is that even when the son becomes CEO, he cannot simply play the role his parents played. The relationship among siblings is much different from that of parents and children. It takes much more time, effort, and communication to maintain sibling support than to gain children's acquiescence. No matter what leadership model emerges for the sibling partnership, the siblings will have a lot of work to do together to make this a success.

Chapter 5

Managing the Outside Risk

Bringing Sibling Spouses into the Fold

Susan was nervous about leaving New York City; she had always enjoyed the big city and fast pace of life and knew this move for her husband Alan to join his family's business was going to be an adjustment on many levels. She was ready to give up her law career—the new baby was making that hard to manage anyway—she just wasn't sure she would be able to fit into the small community where Alan grew up. She didn't know anyone in the area except Alan's family, though everyone seemed to know her, which was unnerving. While Alan's family had always been polite, she felt they didn't really trust her, a feeling cemented when on the day Alan announced their engagement to his family, they sent over legal documents for a prenuptial agreement.

Once they had settled into their home, Susan started longing for the anonymity of the big city, but Alan was "delighted to be home" where folks drop in at any time of day or night, without notice if they are family. While Susan was glad for a support network for the baby, she resented the lack of privacy. In addition, as the family business was a major employer in town, there were a lot of after-hours obligations for both Alan and her, attending networking and social functions where family attendance was not optional. Susan was glad to be meeting so many people, but she often felt folks had an agenda with her that related to her husband's role in the business, rather to her as a person. As a result, even when surrounded by a crowd of people, Susan usually felt lonely, and Alan was simply too busy with work to do much about this.

Finally, Susan could not understand the amount of time Alan was spending with his family, at work and after hours. His parents expected all their adult children to dine at their house every weekend, which often degenerated into lengthy conversations about a business deal or angry words around who was doing a better job of holding up their responsibility as a member of the family at work. Susan knew better than to take sides at dinner, but she could not understand why her husband enjoyed his work when all she ever heard were his complaints about his sister and brother's work ethic. It seemed to Susan that family time for Alan was really just an extension of work time and she started to really question his commitment to living the balanced lifestyle they had promised each other when they were first married.

Susan's story is a composite of the many, many stories we have heard from spouses in business-owning families. Quite simply, it is hard to marry into a family business. The arrival of in-laws in the family system is a significant event; it represents growth in the family and the possibility of a next generation, but it also generates a lot of anxiety. These new family members often make a business-owning family edgy. The perceived danger for family businesses is that an unhappy spouse can threaten a sibling partnership and destroy any sense of team cohesion, in particular if the couple's tension comes from the family member's involvement in the family's business. A spouse can represent a value system that differs from that of the family she or he is joining and may not understand what life in a family owning a business is like. In addition, unless the business is protected by prenuptial and shareholders' agreements, an embittered spouse can gain access to assets and cripple a family company financially if the couple divorces.

While families often focus on the risks, a happy spouse can be a tremendous asset to a sibling partnership and contribute to its strength. No one can guarantee your family member's marital bliss, but good planning around this new stage of life can help. In addition, it is important that the business-owning family can view the situation from the perspective of the in-law. With empathy, understanding, acceptance, and education, families can help spouses support the family business and the sibling partnership. In the interest of building that empathy, let's consider some of the challenges confronting in-laws when they join the family business system:

In-laws often experience culture shock when they enter their new families. Unless they come from a business-owning family themselves—and in our experience, this the case for less than 5 percent of those who marry into a family business—they have little understanding of what to expect. As one new daughter-in-law put it: "The family business is the central topic every time family members get together. If you aren't closely involved in the business, you feel left out." Having the outsiders feel excluded is a challenge that most families in business face, and this sentiment can be even more intense for a person who is also new to the family.

Sometimes in-laws feel overwhelmed by the energy and enthusiasm of the tightly knit families into which they have married. Business-owning families tend to be very involved in one another's lives, both personally and profession-ally. If a new spouse did not grow up in such a tight-knit family, he or she may find this level of involvement suffocating. In addition, even if the spouse is comfortable with the close-knit structure of the new family, he or she may find it difficult to be accepted as a full-fledged member. Very close families may initially resent the arrival of a new member, and that person may be seen as taking up too much of the attention of the family member who married. As a result, there may be more jealousy and resentment toward in-laws in a system like this.

In-laws may struggle with learning about the business. They may feel in a bind about questions: If they don't ask enough questions about the business, the family thinks they lack interest; if they ask too many ques-tions, they are regarded as nosy. They'd like to know more but hesitate asking basic questions for fear of seeming naive or stupid. Moreover, how are they expected to know where their involvement and voice is welcome, and where it oversteps a line unless they receive some guid-ance about these family business boundaries? Not only do spouses need to learn about the business, they need to gain an understanding of the overlap of family and business.

When in-laws side with their husband or wife in a conflict with a parent or sibling, as many spouses naturally do, they may incur the displeasure of the family. Spouses often only hear about issues or frustrations, not about the resolutions, and they only get one side of the story. So, in our earlier example, son Alan may complain to wife Susan that his brother Sam is not pulling his weight on a particular deal or disrespecting him in front of employees. Susan then may develop some resentment toward her brother-in-law or question his competence and worry that her husband is being mistreated. Perhaps Alan fails to mention to Susan Sam's earlier and vital contributions to the project, and he may not tell her about Sam coming in the next day and apologizing for his harsh words. As a result, Susan is left with a biased view of what goes on at the office. Susan feels she is doing the natural thing by wanting to defend her husband, and she may not be aware that she has a very incomplete picture of the situation at work.

In such situations, the family often perceive the spouse as the guilty party, but more often than not the siblings themselves, and secondarily their parents, are the real culprits. If the in-laws become a negative force in a family business, this is often a result of poor behavior or inadequate communication by the siblings and parents. As is made evident in Susan's story, marrying into a business family can be overwhelming for a new family member. The family should recognize the additional burden and expectations that the business puts on all family members and at least prepare a new spouse for this reality.

In addition, a young couple needs some time alone, not because the spouses want to avoid the family or valued traditions, but because they are working to establish their own traditions and boundaries on which they want to build their family. They must be encouraged to truly harmonize as a couple and a nuclear family unit before they can comfortably be a part of the larger family system. The arrival of spouses means you are now both one family and several families. We find healthy family systems maintain a balance between the needs of the individual family units and the needs and expectations of the larger family system.

WHAT CAN SIBLINGS DO?

◆ Prepare your future spouse for the nature of the commitment to the broader family that comes with marrying into your family.

Without scaring off a prospective mate, establish realistic expectations so your future spouse is not surprised by family meetings, reunions, holidays, or whatever commitments your family has made to building unity and relationships with one another outside of work.

- Siblings can also, as part of their code of conduct, make a pact to champion and support one another in front of their spouses. Do not complain about each other to your spouses. Agree that your sibling relationships are precious to you and inviolable and will not be compromised by your marriage relationships and vice versa!

- If you have a problem at work with a sibling, do all you can to settle it at work before you go home and do not take it home with you.

- Make sure you spend time and invest in relationships with your spouse's family. The demands your family makes for "broad family togetherness" will be better understood by your spouse if you also commit to spending time with his or her family.

- As a team and as individuals, work to develop independence from the need for parental approval and decide to make the approval of your siblings the gold standard.

- If relationships are reasonably healthy, include spouses in family meetings of the sibling generation even if you're talking mostly about business issues. This helps build their support for the unity of the sibling team. It helps spouses put individual issues into a broader context, enabling them to see the big picture. It also gives them the opportunity to get information firsthand.

- Develop individual relationships with in-laws. Get to know your brother's wife, your sister's husband. Then, if problems arise, deal with the in-law directly, one-on-one.

WHAT CAN PARENTS DO?

While the suggestions below apply to all family members, they are directed particularly at the founders in their capacity as leaders of the family. In our experience, the parents of the siblings have a powerful role to play in reaching out to the spouses their children bring into the family and in helping these individuals feel truly welcome.

- Take time to welcome your new family member into the fold. We find families that take the time to explicitly bring new family members on board see far fewer conflicts or problems with in-laws in this next generation. While it may seem odd to orient a person to your family, the reality is that there is a lot to master for people joining a business-owning family. New spouses need to learn the history of the family and the business, gain at least a "cocktail-party" level of knowledge of the company; they must learn the core family values (and, hopefully, assimilate these) and how these values affect personal and business conduct by all. They should also learn about any existing family business policies and much more. In addition, new in-laws may need to learn about family ownership of the business and what ownership means. Joint ownership can impact family interaction in surprising ways, such as motivating family members to invest in their relationships outside of work and pursue joint estate planning, to name just two examples. The better in-laws understand the reasons for these activities, the more likely they are to buy in and find ways to be supportive.
- Invest in educating in-laws. The more in-laws understand about the business and the realities of day-to-day trade-offs and choices, the more likely they are to see the big picture when something affects their spouse. We strongly encourage the greatest possible transparency and sharing that the family can tolerate. For example, we recommend discussing issues such as compensation for family members in an open manner.
- Be empathetic regarding the difficulty of joining your family. Do not view any requests for boundaries on the part of a new spouse as a rejection of your family, but rather as a normal need to create some appropriate limits and privacy.
- Play up the strengths of your children's spouses. Learn about their interests and passions so that the family can share in these

as well. Ask them to share their valued family traditions and try to incorporate some of their history into the family's broader system. Show appreciation of spouses' wisdom, talents, and traditions.

- Put limits on shoptalk. Require some family time during which discussing the family business is explicitly off-limits.
- If prenuptials are required in your family make sure they are applied equally. It's important that all in-laws understand that prenuptial agreements apply to all family members and have the reasons for their existence explained.

WHAT IN-LAWS CAN DO

- Recognize that a sibling partnership is time-consuming and demanding. Being a part of such a team is one of the most difficult tasks your spouse could undertake. He or she will need your patience and understanding.
- Don't take sides or serve as an advocate for your spouse. If you think your husband or wife is being treated unfairly in the business, let your mate work it out.
- Learn all you can about your spouse's family business and about family businesses in general. Many colleges and universities across the country have programs that family members can attend. Read the entire Family Business Leadership series (see p. ii) and subscribe to the free online *Family Business Advisor* newsletter. Magazines such as *Family Business* or other business magazines can also be useful.
- Develop friendships with members of your spouse's family. This enables the family to know you as a person and helps build trust.
- During family business meetings, don't present personal perspectives on business issues. It is not appropriate, for example, to complain that your husband's boss does not appreciate how

hard he works. Evaluating executives is the job of the business's management and board.

One of the challenges for spouses coming into a business-owning family is that the family can be a tight-knit group with long-established traditions, inside jokes, norms of conduct, etc. As a new spouse, you may feel like you are back in middle school trying to break into an "in-crowd" clique that isn't really looking for newcomers. It is not that the family intentionally wants to reject you; family members are merely very protective of the warm and loving bonds that have been built over decades, and they aren't sure how you are going to fit in. As a new in-law, you need to work on not taking this personally, and the family needs to work at being as inclusive as possible while respecting the new family member's need for some boundaries and privacy as well. We cannot emphasize enough that spouses should be included in family meetings and that the extended family should find ways to have fun together by sharing family vacations, retreats, holidays, etc. to begin to build memories and family bonds that also include the siblings' spouses.

Including spouses in family meetings helps them to begin to feel like a full-fledged member of the family. The more the family can include the in-laws, the more they will appreciate why the family's commitment to the enterprise is important, and the role they can play in upholding the values, educating the next generation, and generally supporting the broader mission of the family. Moreover, when in-laws are at the meetings, they get messages and information that are not filtered through their husbands or wives, and they are able to form their own opinions. They also get to see their spouses in action, so they're not just depending on the tales that the spouses tell about themselves.

When spouses are involved in events that are just for fun or that represent the work of the family, family members and in-laws get to know one another better, see each other's different dimensions, and grow in appreciation of one another. All of this supports the sibling team and lays a foundation for the eventual success of the cousin generation to follow.

A FEW WORDS ABOUT PRENUPTIAL AGREEMENTS

For many families who own businesses, prenuptials are normal and often a good idea. But be aware of the following caveats:

1. As far as the business-owning family is concerned, the primary purpose of a prenuptial agreement should be to preserve the ownership of the business within the direct lineal descendants of the founders. A prenuptial agreement should focus on ownership of stock in the family business or the family's shared wealth. Any issues to be addressed related to personal assets should be left up to the couples themselves. Note also that if the family's primary concerns are related to protecting access to ownership interests, carefully crafted ownership agreements may make prenuptial agreements unnecessary.

2. Plan ahead. Start thinking and talking about prenuptial agreements before any child has a serious relationship. Thinking about prenuptials after an engagement can create bitterness. We know of one family where the faxed prenuptial agreement response to the engagement announcement led to years of resentment. Thinking about prenuptials after marriage (called a post-nuptial) adds an entire new level of complexity. The best practice is for the family to agree before any engagements that prenuptial agreements will be the policy. The younger generation should be prepared by appropriate experts to understand why such agreements are necessary and be able to communicate that understanding to potential future spouses.

3. Require prenuptial agreements of all family members. Don't require an agreement just because a son is marrying a woman the family does not like. By stipulating prenuptials across the board and explaining to future in-laws the reasons behind the policy, there is a better chance of creating and maintaining goodwill.

EXHIBIT 5.1.   Premarital agreements are more likely to hold up in court when...

- **Full disclosure is made.** Each person should provide the other with a complete description of his or her finances, including assets and debts, and a statement of expected gifts, inheritances, and potential acquisitions and earnings.

  NOTE: This can create issues in families where full disclosure has not yet been made to the next generation about their assets. An impending wedding sometimes forces the issue of disclosure to the children, which may catch some families unprepared. While there are some situations (e.g., serious substance abuse) where adult children are not ready to handle this information, typically, the arrival of your children to the stage of marriage is a signal that a whole host of new adult responsibilities may be coming their way, including a more complete knowledge of their financial and ownership situation. Do not allow your anxiety about disclosing financial information to your children prevent you from drafting a prenuptial that will hold up in court. This highlights again why it is important to plan well in advance, so that your family is in a position to share information with the adult children on your timetable, not feeling rushed or pressured by external events.

- **Each party is represented by his or her own attorney to ensure** that each party receives independent counsel and adequate financial disclosure prior to signing. We have seen many cases where the business-owning family is the one to defray the costs of this legal support to the intended spouse, but the attorney understands that the future in-law is his or her client.

- The agreement is fair and consciable. The wealthier party, for example, cannot cause the spouse to become a public charge by removing all support and other property rights. We have seen families carefully provide for a spouse in the case of death or divorce. Once again, the required thought and effort involved highlight the importance of planning.

- Both parties enter the agreement voluntarily. Both must be of legal age, and the signing must not be the result of coercion, duress, or undue influence.

- The contract is signed well in advance of the marriage. Not to keep stressing the importance of planning, but last-minute signing might be viewed as "under duress."

- Couples adequately define property as "separate," "marital," or "community." Separate property is any property brought to the marriage or received by gift or inheritance during the marriage and, in the event of divorce, is not subject to being shared with a spouse. Marital or community property is any property that is acquired during a marriage and is subject to an "equitable" division upon divorce.

Chapter 6

Developing the Sibling Partnership

Successful transition to sibling generation leadership requires preparation and effort by all stakeholders of the family business. The complexity of the sibling stage in a family business typically requires adjustments in management, business governance, and the family's decision making. Ideally, the senior generation works with the next generation to plan for these changes. Too often, however, generations clash rather than collaborate. Founders may not realize the difference between the owners' role and management's role because they have been doing both, and they may not always understand how differently their children will have to deal with decision making. In addition, many founders resist letting go of authority and will struggle with change of any kind. As a result, sibling team building often falls to the siblings themselves. This chapter will provide some guidance on the core elements the siblings should address in developing their partnership.

SHARED PURPOSE AND LIMITED AUTONOMY

Establishing a well-functioning sibling team requires siblings to commit to a shared purpose, actively seeking common ground. Defining this shared purpose is work the siblings can do together, whether their parents are supportive and actively involved in the transition process or not, and this is a great way for the siblings to begin to take some initiative as suggested in chapter 3. It is important for siblings to clarify their shared purpose by answering the following questions:

- Why do we want to be in business together?
- What does business ownership mean to each of us?
- What are our values, our vision, and our goals related to our business and its success?

Finding the answers and sharing them allows siblings to find their voice and purpose and sets the stage for many other decisions they need to make.

The success of the sibling generation depends on the team's ability to focus on something larger than the concerns of each sibling, such as the good of the business or the family or their mission. This implies some loss of autonomy because decisions need to be made in collaboration with others, bearing in mind the priorities, preferences, and concerns of a range of stakeholders. If some or all of the siblings are hoping one day to get to "make all the decisions like Dad does," they will be disappointed. In order to be successful, a sibling partnership must be a collaboration of partners, not a test of wills. Like any meaningful partnership (e.g., marriage), the sibling partnership can only be successful if there is some give-and-take; the siblings must be ready to give up some of their individual freedom if the partnership is to work. As one of our clients stated in the course of a discussion about his ambition related to business leadership in his family: "What role I end up playing is far less important than how successful we manage to be as a team."

We also find having a larger goal enables many a family to work through conflicts and rivalries and get beyond self-interest and ego. When a sibling team having difficulties focuses primarily on its conflicts, problems may seem intractable. Those who seek common ground take the time to understand why they're together doing what they do. First, they celebrate and appreciate their common blessings. They focus on their shared values, vision, and goals that serve as the foundation on which they build. Buttressed by what they share, they refuse to allow conflicts to tear them apart. Only after affirming their shared commitments do they attend to their differences and say, "Let's work on those."

In addition to articulating a shared purpose, sibling teams grow in effectiveness as all members increase in the ability to:

- respect others and demonstrate that respect,
- know themselves and the boundaries between themselves and others,
- clarify and take responsibility for their own feelings (As one member of a team said when he was disappointed with a particular decision, "It is not everybody's job to cater to how I feel and make me feel better. It is my job to deal with my own feelings."),
- understand everyone's goals and help find ways to attain them,
- accept and tolerate each other's differences and avoid being judgmental of each other's lifestyle or choice of spouse,
- empathize with, but don't assume knowledge of others' views and learn to listen to each other's perspectives.

Finally, we find it helps to think in terms of being one family. "Look," said one of three sisters struggling to develop an effective ownership team, "let's always remember four things: we love each other; we are all doing our best; we don't want to hurt each other; and we will be a whole lot stronger together than any of us can be separately." As another business owner put it, he and his sisters agree to agree. They feel that in the long run unity is more important than any particular decision. This applies to all business and family issues that will confront the siblings over the years. If the sibling generation establishes and lives the norm of one family, a strong foundation will be set for generations to come.

VALUES AND VISION

Jim O'Doul grew up in a small town and had little education but a strong work ethic. Finding no opportunity where he was, he moved to a part of the country that was growing, following an uncle into construction-related trades. Over time Jim developed a following of customers due to his hard work and creative solutions, leveraging these into a business of his own. Four decades later this business has grown to several hundred million in sales, employing hundreds of people. While Jim is still a force of nature, he had been looking to slow down when some investors came along with a handsome offer to buy the business.

Neither Jim nor his family (four adult children) need the money, they live well and enjoy working. However, this was not a decision to be taken lightly, and as he had started transitioning ownership to his children, Jim asked his children whether the family should sell or not, and why. "After all," he told them, "it is your future." Initially the siblings struggled with these discussions. One was trying to prove to his father he could do sophisticated business analysis. Another got caught up in the morality of having "too much" money and of putting local jobs at risk. One couldn't conceive of selling "daddy's legacy," and the fourth favored selling because the proceeds could be conservatively invested, virtually eliminating business risk. On the whole, they were getting nowhere.

To address the impasse, the siblings met without their father but with a facilitator. They spent time clarifying their shared values and determining what ownership of the business meant to each of them individually and what it meant for their family. They gave strong consideration to what they could do together or separately with the funds from a sale and realized that their dreams were better achieved through ongoing ownership of the business. They realized they shared a strong commitment to the local community and believed that as stewards of the enterprise they could be a force for growth, providing good jobs and a strong economic base that would fund better schools. In addition, the family had a long tradition of involvement in civic and religious organizations that they feared would fall by the wayside if they sold their interest. Finally, while they were unlikely to move from the area, they realized nothing would tie their children to this part of the country if the business were not there as an anchor. They decided not to sell but committed to each other, their parents, and their key non-family executives that they would be the most knowledgeable and most accountable ownership team possible.

Families typically are bound together through shared history, traditions, and values. For families with a deep legacy of faith, these common values may be easier to identify than for families with a more secular orientation. While secular families may not be as likely as religious ones to have clear labels for their shared values, they do have beliefs of fundamental significance that guide their decision making and priorities. Taking the time to identify and reflect on these shared values helps siblings in a partnership build on their shared purpose and clarify the priorities of their partnership. This sets the context for many other decisions.

Values are the bedrock of family and business culture. They deeply influence decisions and priorities. For example, while both integrity and innovation are good values that can anchor a business, a business based on the core value of integrity might make different choices than one guided by a core value of innovation. What is important is that the siblings agree on values and have a common vision for the future direction of the enterprise. The siblings must articulate how their shared values impact their vision for family collaboration in the business and in any other joint endeavors or priorities they hope to pursue (see *Family Business Values: How to Assure a Legacy of Continuity and Success* in the Family Business Leadership series, listed on p. ii, for more information on values).

ESTABLISHING MISSION AND GOALS

While shared purpose, priorities, and a vision are important to answer the big fundamental questions mentioned above, siblings must also think tactically about how they hope to make their vision a reality. What are the specific goals and objectives toward which they will work together?

Initially, the siblings may only be able to set goals for their partnership, such as developing the policies they will use for decision making in the future. Another example of a goal they could establish on their own might be to organize a family retreat as a way to realize their core value of sustaining family unity. Once the sibling team is in a position of authority, the siblings may also get involved with goals for the business. For example, if family members are oriented to growth of the enterprise, they may decide together whether that is better pursued through acquisition or through organic growth. While each family will have its own mission and goals for the business, what successful sibling partnerships have in common are processes for making such decisions. We encourage siblings to have regular meetings to discuss future roles, policies, and goals and to work on communication skills as a team to reduce and resolve conflicts and maximize long-term effectiveness.

DETERMINE YOUR RULES

Four siblings have developed themselves into a strong team by meeting quarterly (with their spouses) for more than two decades to make decisions together. Over the years, they have spent time drafting policies that help them navigate complex issues. For example, they set the expectation that their children will complete college and two years of work experience before joining the business full-time. They also set guidelines that affect their own roles, deciding to hire the person who is best qualified for every position in the business regardless of family membership. This policy was tested when one of their spouses was in the running for a top executive role and was not selected. Though he was disappointed, he was comfortable with the decision (having been integrally involved with the decision to hire the best-qualified person, whether a family member or not for this role), felt the outcome was fair, and continues to be a key contributor the business.

In addition to formulating and clarifying their shared purpose, siblings can draft guidelines that will govern their conduct as a family and as business partners. They determine the process for making decisions, such as who gets a voice, voting rules, and areas of individual or collective authority, etc. They can develop a code of conduct on how they will conduct themselves in public, demonstrate respect for one another and how they will speak about each other to others, especially to spouses, parents, and members of the community.

By developing policies regarding these matters, siblings are agreeing on solutions to problems in advance. Doing so ensures consistency, fairness, and objectivity while depersonalizing decisions that could otherwise cause serious conflicts. By discussing these complicated issues in detail and in advance, siblings strengthen their communication and problem-solving skills. The following policies will benefit the family and the business at the sibling stage:

Employment/participation. *Families who emphasize that family members prepare themselves through education and experience to make a real contribution to the business typically find greater harmony and success. Many families also develop policies with regard to in-laws working in the business, part-time employment, and career development once a family member has joined the business. Policies governing qualifications for participation in the family business become increasingly important as the third generation becomes old enough to think about joining the business.*

Many families that develop comprehensive policy guides for the business also set standards for family members' participation on the board of directors. Several families that we've worked with have determined that to serve on the board of one's family business, a family member must have the qualifications that would make him or her eligible to serve on the board of another, unrelated company.

Compensation. *Open, explicit compensation arrangements are very helpful; they tell family members what they can expect and what is expected of them. Compensation policies also often address benefits, perks, and time off. (For more on this topic, see* Family Business Compensation *in the* Family Business Leadership *series listed on p. ii.)*

Shareholders' agreements. *These are contracts among shareholders that specify rights with respect to stock ownership under various circumstances, such as death, retirement, voluntary or involuntary separation from the business, divorce, or in case the shareholder wants to sell his or her shares. They enable a family to plan for stressful events. For example, these agreements may restrict who can be an owner of the business, or they may obligate a shareholder to sell shares when a triggering event occurs, such as retirement or disability.*

Exit and redemption. Family members at any stage may desire the freedom to opt out of ownership. However, the capital requirements of the business may make such flexibility highly problematic. Ideally, sibling owners should continue to own shares through their own choice and be able to let go of their shares without feeling that they are selling out or leaving their family. How to balance business capital needs and individual financial freedom is one challenge siblings must be ready to confront, and it should inform their thinking as they consider policies regarding liquidity.

Other policies that siblings might consider putting in place include the following:

- Retirement age
- Dividends
- Company loans to family members
- Ownership rights and responsibilities
- Conflicts of interest
- Ethics
- Publicity
- Assistance for family members in need.

Siblings will find it valuable to revisit major issues from time to time, such as compensation, participation, corporate vision, and buy-sell agreements to see if the policies governing them continue to be appropriate and still have the group's support. (See *Developing Family Business Policies: Your Guide to the Future* in the Family Business Leadership series, listed on p. ii, for more on policy development).

MANAGING THE INSIDER-OUTSIDER DILEMMA

Among other important challenges sibling teams must address how they will manage the dilemma of insiders versus outsiders. In some cases, all siblings in the second generation work in the family business, but often siblings do not choose to work in the business they will one day co-own. For example, one of your siblings may be passionate about teaching or aspire to a career in the military or simply is not business minded. Ideally, the family members working in the business are passionate about their work and want to contribute all they can to the success of the family business. No one wants business partners who are working in the business primarily because they have no other choice or feel obligated to do so.

In some cases ownership is restricted to siblings working in the business. Increasingly, however, siblings who do not work in the company own shares through gifting or inheritance. An appropriate balance must be struck between owners in the business and those not in the business. The need to find this balance underscores the importance of clarifying the distinctions between ownership and management decisions. The process requires a good understanding and respect for boundaries and demands strong communication skills. Sibling owners who do not work in the business must understand that they cannot tell management how to do its job, but it is vitally important that the siblings who work in the business realize they are accountable to all owners. All owners should work together to develop a common vision, goals, and understanding of the rewards of both employment and ownership. Specific actions sibling teams should pursue include the following:

- Communicate with and educate all owners about the business.
- Make sure all owners are involved in key ownership decisions, particularly those related to strategy, succession, and major financial issues.
- Share power; siblings leading the business should encourage others to be in charge of family meetings, philanthropy, recording the family history, or other areas of responsibility.
- Adopt an attitude of "we're all in it together" instead of thinking of yourselves as different branches of a family. Consider yourselves a tribe.
- Promote, support, and champion siblings not working in the business just as you do those ones working in the company.
- Involve everyone in drafting policies like the ones discussed above.

ESTABLISH A LEADERSHIP STRUCTURE

The siblings must also grapple with how to lead and govern themselves. We strongly recommend that the siblings all have a voice in choosing the leadership system and selecting leaders from among their group. Decisions on these issues require a high level of trust and a good understanding of the family and business systems. To deal with them effectively, the siblings must have had ample practice in collaboration and in making team decisions on smaller matters. Determining the ideal future leadership for the business requires understanding the challenges and opportunities the company will likely face in the future. These considerations will impact the design of business governance structures providing management oversight (more on this in chapter 7). Finally, siblings should consider how the family's goals and needs may change over time and determine how best to provide family leadership to meet those needs.

It is best if sibling teams have multiple leaders. Those best suited to take the helm of the business are often not the optimal family leaders. Different skills are required for these jobs. Just as the company grows in complexity and faces new challenges in this next generation, so does the family. Multiple households, inclusion of in-laws, a growing third generation, diversity among siblings, and a host of other challenges and opportunities will require thoughtful, engaged leadership. In our experience families pay far too little attention to the leadership needs of the family. Often, this is because they are unaware of all that their mother may have done in the founding generation as the family's "Chief Emotional Officer" to keep relationships strong and the family united.

Family leadership is often more difficult than business leadership. More sibling partnerships fail because of family conflict or apathy than because of business troubles—and yet, far more effort and attention tends to be given to business leadership matters. Family leaders must have excellent communication skills and be deeply trusted as they do not benefit from the authority of a formal hierarchy or the resources and support that are available to business leaders. Instead, family leaders must primarily rely on extensive communication, relationship building, and consensus-building skills to ensure family cohesion and progress toward the family's goals.

Many families also struggle to identify appropriate leaders for the business. What if the most qualified person isn't the firstborn son who has been with the business the longest? What if no one in the family wants the job? What if there are several qualified family members? What if there is a better qualified manager who is not a family member? While policies (e.g., we will hire the most qualified person for the position) can help in making the leadership choice, determining the policies that will set these boundaries can be a challenge. Some families will want to reserve the top leadership spot for a family member but may have to find a way to ensure they do not lose better qualified key executives who will be needed to support the new CEO. What if the family CEO will have some siblings reporting to him or her in this new role? How will equal owners manage the unequal hierarchy of their work roles? What if the siblings want to work as a leadership team or co-CEOs instead of one CEO?

While there are no formulas for ideal family business leadership that will fit every case, the business leader who succeeds the founder must have the technical and management skills needed to lead the business *and* must have the trust of the family. Ideally, this person is the best-qualified leader in the enterprise and has close relationships with the sibling ownership team. The sibling generation often uses the help of a carefully selected board of directors in order to structure business leadership and make effective decisions about top-level executives in the family business.

The leaders of the family business in the successor generation also often adopt a philosophy of servant-leadership rather than taking a directive approach (especially if there are other siblings who are also involved in leading the business). Servant leaders "serve" the constituencies they lead, understanding their goals and helping them to maximize fulfillment. If there are siblings not working in the business, the sibling leader of the business should be especially mindful of communication between management and ownership. Understanding how to garner support for executive action is the mark of a strong and effective leader in the successor generation. Mutual accountability marks the success of the sibling generation.

While most businesses choose one operational leader, we also see a growing number of family businesses that choose to take a team approach to leadership, using an "office of the president" rather than one CEO. When the leadership group has complementary skills and excellent communication, this can work. However, having several leaders adds complexity that requires thorough analysis and planning. This option should never just be a way of avoiding making a tough choice between leadership candidates.

EXHIBIT 6.1.   Essentials for co-CEOs

- Each successor-candidate is very capable, competent, and prepared for leadership.
- Candidates share fundamental goals, values, and levels of commitment.
- In addition to general leadership responsibilities, each potential cosuccessor has specific areas of responsibility.
- Candidates have solid relationships with one another.
- They demonstrate the ability to process and resolve differences constructively.
- An experienced board of directors, including respected outsiders, holds the CEO team accountable, gives perspective, and provides a safety net if leaders reach an impasse.

Chapter 7

Building the Business and Family Systems to Support the Sibling Partnership

The appropriate management structure of an enterprise at the sibling stage will vary depending on the business, industry, markets served, number of employees, etc. It is beyond the scope of this book to prescribe optimal management structures, but it is almost certainly necessary to move the company away from the hub-and-spoke model of management that is common of many businesses at the founding stage. Hopefully, the company has grown to a size where running all decisions through a single-decision maker is impractical. At this stage we often also find the business faces complex choices, such as whether to take on debt to build a second plant or expand into another area or acquire a local competitor, that benefit from the wisdom and challenging questions a board of directors can put to management.

While the siblings can take a lot of steps as detailed in the previous chapter to establish their team, they may not be as free to make the changes needed in the management and oversight systems of the business, or these changes may come very slowly. If the founder is still active in the business and highly controlling, there may be an unwillingness to change how decisions are made in the short term. Unfortunately, this inflexibility can have serious consequences because a management team that has had few opportunities to build skills or confidence as decision makers will be weak. This can create challenges for the siblings in the long run if these managers fail to adapt once the siblings are empowered to distribute responsibility to a broader group of leaders in the company.

PROFESSIONALIZING THE BUSINESS

We believe that as much as possible systems should be in place before they are needed. In an ideal situation, the founding generation is aware that the company has outgrown its original management structure and has started the process of professionalizing the company as part of the overall process of continuity planning. The founders' input or approval of this process can make a significant positive impact as other stakeholders will resist change less if the revered founder sanctions the new ways. Unfortunately, founders' more frequently resist letting go of their authority, and this makes it unusual to see changes welcomed. Founders who take on a productive role in this evolution do an enormous favor to their successors and their enterprise.

Professionalizing a family business means not only constructing more diffuse and formalized decision-making processes but also putting into place the people who have skills suited for larger organizations. Leaders in a more developed organization must have the skills to make a business case to a board of directors, for example, for investment in a new plant. In the preceding generation, this decision might have been more driven by the intuition of the founder. Companies at the later stage often need to also formalize their human resource function, drafting job descriptions and ensuring that both family and non-family executives are compensated reasonably. Financial reporting is another example of a business process that needs to be more sophisticated at the sibling stage, both to address the needs of the owners and to better support opportunities in the business itself.

These important changes impact the skills needed to operate the business, which will affect any employee who aspires to a leadership role in the enterprise, whether a family member or not. As the sibling team begins to make the decisions and take the actions necessary to assure the success of a growing company, it needs to be sensitive to its relationship with key non-family executives. Some of these executives may feel threatened by the processes of change from one generation to the next. Thus, forward-thinking sibling teams consider management development of non-family executives as well as their own roles for the future in their continuity planning. The larger the enterprise you have and hope to develop, the broader and deeper you need your executive bench to be. Developing a cadre of talented leaders will be critical to the success of the business in the sibling generation and beyond.

During the transition period when both the founding and sibling generation are involved in the business, it is not unusual for non-family executives to assume that a competition is going on among the siblings and to look to the parents for clues as to who the successor really is. Siblings may even discover that non-family executives are actively supporting one sibling over another. No matter what leadership structure is established in the sibling generation, it is critical that the family speak with one voice. Even if they are working in different locations, siblings need to act as a unit in their relationships with non-family executives. The siblings need to get together and talk about day-to-day management issues, such as how they're going to relate to the vice president of sales. "Do we offer encouragement? Is this a person we really want to promote in the future?" Through such discussion, the team can become united in its position and avoid sending mixed messages to non-family executives.

To ensure all lines of communication are open, and that the owner-managers are consistently speaking with one voice it is important for all siblings in the business to touch base regarding important decisions on a regular basis.

Having formal structures in a family business will seem strange at first for the family that hasn't had them. Families often prefer to think of themselves as being spontaneous and informal. But when a business is large enough to take the siblings in and will grow larger because of the contribution they make, it needs the order and framework for future growth that structure, policies, and procedures supply. It may take a while to learn to use these new tools effectively, but once this is mastered, everyone will wonder how the business—and the family—ever managed without them.

BUSINESS GOVERNANCE

In addition to changing the management structure of the enterprise, the sibling stage is often the first time companies consider a formal board of directors. When the siblings become a significant voice in the management of the company, establishing a higher authority provides structure and accountability to the entire enterprise. Best practice suggests that a board have several respected, independent, and experienced directors selected from leaders of other well-run, successful companies.

While many founders resist putting a board in place, those who have done so report that it is one of the most valuable investments they have ever made. Especially as the company faces its first generational transition, a solid board can provide guidance on the management overhaul required; managerial, organizational and strategic change; empathy and support for the CEO; the discipline to keep the succession process on track; and leadership continuity through the entire volatile process.

A board becomes a forum that makes for constructive discourse on the biggest decisions or challenges facing the enterprise. Independent outsiders can serve as a moderating force and help the siblings resolve differences and encourage them to become independent of the parents. The outsiders can mentor the siblings, encouraging them to form themselves into an effective ownership and/or management team. An active board serves as an additional resource to the siblings, gives them feedback, and provides objectivity. Objectivity can be particularly valuable when it comes to navigating sensitive topics such as compensation or even opportunities for leadership advancement within the sibling group. These directors can also play a role in educating the siblings who are not active in the business and help them understand the realities of a business as well as their role in it.

The board provides incentive for the business's managers to discipline themselves and accept a certain level of accountability, thus providing a good complement to the more professional management structures described above. The board also serves as a check and balance on siblings and parents alike. It can make sure the siblings aren't making unwise decisions and can encourage the parents to be patient even if their kids make some mistakes. Because the board is there, everyone tends to behave better. The board facilitates consensus, healing, and proactive behavior.

PROFESSIONAL ADVISORS

Whether or not a long-standing board has been in place, over time, the sibling partnership should develop its own set of professional advisors and independent directors. Just as there is a transition of leadership and ownership in the business, a transition of advisors is necessary. In some cases, the advisors themselves facilitate this transition. For example, a 67-year-old senior partner who has always been dad's lawyer may be wise enough to introduce his 35-year-old partner-to-be to begin developing a relationship with the sibling team.

The siblings should collectively choose their professional advisors and outside directors. The advisors should represent or work with the group as a unit and see it as a team. In selecting advisors, the team should go through a formal process: generating a set of necessary criteria and characteristics, developing a list of candidates and carefully evaluating them, and then making an informed choice. Those chosen by the ownership team should view the owners, not the business, as the client. Too often, advisors who see themselves as serving the business are most responsive to the CEO, who after all, is giving the advisor work and approving the bills.

SKILLS AND KNOWLEDGE

While many business founders achieve great success with limited education, it does not necessarily follow that their children can play as central a role in the business with as little formal education. This is not to suggest every next generation family member needs a graduate or even college degree; however, it does mean that some roles in the business are best filled by individuals who have knowledge typically gained through schooling. In addition, we believe all siblings, whether active in the business or not, need to develop basic financial literacy as well as familiarity with the enterprise to be effective owners and stewards. If you do not have a family member with the skills to oversee the cash flow and other financial matters in your business, all future owners must at a minimum have enough knowledge to understand, and ask good questions about, the financial reports professionals will provide.

In addition to learning the skills they need to fulfill their fiduciary duty as owners, we find the most effective sibling teams are those who have invested time and energy in communication skills and team development exercises. This can include practice with difficult conversations, listening skills, or learning about one another's communication styles. Some siblings like to do ropes courses or similar team-building adventures to learn and practice working together. Many sibling teams we work with enjoy doing some personality testing to better understand their similarities and differences. The choice of tool or approach for these efforts should be adapted to your family. What you choose to do is less important than the ongoing commitment to work on these skills.

FAMILY MEETINGS

Finally, we strongly encourage siblings to initiate family meetings. In our experience, regular family meetings are one of the three most important predictors of long-term family business success (the other two are putting a board in place and engaging in regular strategic planning). These meetings ideally include all siblings, spouses, perhaps older children from the third generation, and parents. Held at least once a year, these get-togethers provide the entire family with the opportunity to talk about such topics as the future, philanthropy, estate planning, education, family history, and much more. Many find this is the right forum to provide the whole family with a basic overview of the performance and broad plans of the business. Keeping family members who are not shareholders current on major changes in the company helps them feel engaged and respected and can help avoid embarrassing situations such as when neighbors at a child's soccer match are more current on company affairs than these family members are!

More important than company updates are the opportunities for family sharing, learning, and bonding. In particular if siblings have moved to different parts of the country, it can be essential to carve out time for regular family to get-togethers. Though the third generation may still be a long way from the business, planting the seeds of family pride, strong bonds, and a commitment to shared purpose early on will stand the family in good stead for the long term. Family meetings can be a great place to discuss challenges that confront the whole family, such as raising children with wealth. Some families like to work on philanthropic projects together, finding ways to give back to the community while building memories and a sense of shared purpose that goes beyond the company. However you choose to spend your time together, the most important elements of a family meeting are that they should include as broad a family group as possible and be held regularly, at least annually (see *Family Meetings: How to Build a Strong Family and a Stronger Business* in the Family Business Leadership series, which is listed on p. ii).

Making regular family meetings a reality requires devoted and competent leadership. While it seems simple to get the family together, the logistics of managing calendars and developing an agenda that balances learning, sharing, and fun in a way that resonates for the whole family is no small feat! As families grow and the goals of the family expand, some families choose to organize the work of the family through a family council, so that not too much falls only on the shoulders of one family leader. A family council will typically organize the family meetings and may have committees to handle the tasks the family wants to pursue at this stage, which could include education, philanthropy, drafting a family constitution, and many more. For example, as the third generation starts to come of age, the family may want to increase its commitment to education of current and future shareholders and start a process for the third generation to begin its collaboration. Through this work and much more, the sibling partnership's family leadership sets the tone for future generations.

EXHIBIT 7.1.   A "to-do list" for sibling team success

- ◆ **Shared sense of purpose.** The duties and burdens of ownership are acceptable because business continuity has significant meaning for every team member.
- ◆ **An independent, outside board.** The best forum for debate and the best possible insurance policy, independent outsiders are a well-established part of the company's governing structure.
- ◆ **Siblings' code of conduct.** The team has explicitly agreed and committed in writing to how it will make decisions, resolve conflict, treat each other, deal with the press and the public, conduct business affairs openly and ethically, and relate to each other.
- ◆ **Proven success at conflict resolution.** All team members trust that serious problems can be overcome without the intervention of their parents.
- ◆ **Experience with open disclosure.** Each knows and accepts past and present salary and perks arrangements. All should know about any parental support and gifting.
- ◆ **Method of future compensation.** A process is in place to set future salaries, bonuses, and dividends and to audit perks and financial relationships with the business and each other.
- ◆ **Participation agreement.** All understand who can work in the business and who can own stock, including consideration for spouses, children, stepchildren, other relatives, etc.

- **Familiarity and comfort with outside directors and key advisors.** All members of the sibling team have good personal relationships with the directors, lawyers, accountants, and other important consultants.
- **Consensus on future of key non-family executives.** The siblings all respect and understand the contributions of key non-family executives and support the development of all talent that helps make the business successful.
- **Completed, known estate plans.** These arrangements assure security to spouses and children and have been finalized and shared with each other.
- **Redemption and exit plan.** A system that permits someone to exit and sell shares (including the pricing and terms) is in place. (Some families deliberately make exit impossible. If so, the arrangement should be legally binding and all should pledge to uphold it for the reasons it was chosen.)

Chapter 8

Sticky Issues and Predictable Bumps in the Road

While proactively planning for the rise of the sibling generation will improve the odds of a smooth intergenerational transition, its accomplishment requires hard work, tenacity, and patience. There will be bumps in the road and roadblocks. We have alluded to some of these challenges throughout this book, but let's take a closer look at some of the most common and serious obstacles that an evolving sibling team may encounter.

THE FOUNDER WON'T LET GO OR "RETIRES" BUT KEEPS SWOOPING BACK IN

There are countless articles and numerous books that address the challenges business founders face in letting go of the leadership of their business. While all stakeholders should appreciate the difficulty involved and have empathy for the founder, founders must also be honest with themselves and others about their intentions in this process. If the founder plans to keep control until death, the siblings should be informed and make their own choices accordingly. Some siblings may choose a path outside the business. Other sibling groups will collaborate with their parents. In either case, we advise siblings to come together to consider common elements of their future as family, prospective owners, and potential business leaders.

In some respects the "boomerang" CEO is worse than one who won't let go. The CEO's frequent return leads to confusion among all stakeholders about who is really in charge. Successful transition from the founder to the sibling team is made more difficult if the founder regularly returns to participate in company decisions or intervene with employees. Such actions undermine the credibility of new leaders and compromise the sibling partnership. As is well demonstrated by the example below, the founders can undercut their children out of anxiety or just by falling into old habits. Such incursions can best be resisted if the sibling team can close ranks and stick together.

> In a printing company we'll call Hibbard Graphics, Dad learned his three kids were considering purchasing an expensive German press. While he had put them in charge and begun semiretirement, he thought buying the press would be a huge mistake. It was too costly, and the company was not doing the kind of printing that would require such a machine. Dad scoffed at the kids' argument that a press like this would boost Hibbard Graphics beyond its competitors and enable it to take on many kinds of jobs it had been incapable of doing before. He was sure that before they knew it, they would be in debt way over their heads and that the contracts they envisioned just wouldn't materialize.

> Dad thought he knew how he could head off catastrophe. He convinced Mom to try to talk their daughter, Elena, out of the idea. Mom and Elena had an especially good relationship, and Dad was sure Mom could persuade Elena that the purchase was a bad idea. Dad himself would collar Stefan, the younger son; they usually saw eye-to-eye. And if Dad could convince Stefan and Mom could convince Elena, then Rob, the older son, would have to give in.

> A great surprise was in store for Dad. Stefan welcomed him warmly and listened for a few minutes while his father tried to persuade him of the foolishness of buying the press. "Dad," he said, "it makes me uncomfortable to have you speaking to me about this privately. Rob, Elena, and I are committed to working as a team. Why don't you come and talk to all

three of us at our executive committee meeting next week? We'll put you on the agenda. We want to hear your views, and eventually we'll make a decision. But it will be a team decision." And, as Mom reported to Dad, she had a similar experience during her visit with Elena.

THE TWO GENERATIONS CANNOT AGREE ON THE BEST PATH FORWARD

The Hibbard case also illustrates the challenge when the two generation are not in agreement on strategy, tactics, or pivotal capital investments but are in some form of power-sharing arrangement. In fact, sometimes the inability of the two generations to see eye-to-eye can lead the senior generation to slow down the process of transitioning authority. In addition, while the founders may be willing to let go of day-to-day management, if their financial security is still vested in the business, they will probably struggle before allowing the siblings free reign on bigger issues such as expanding into new markets or taking on significant debt.

Avoiding misunderstandings and backsliding requires establishing clear expectations for communication and decision-making boundaries in advance. Some founders will want to be consulted only on decisions above a certain dollar amount, but others may want to be kept in the loop on all matters for a certain period of time. Ensuring that communication works to everyone's satisfaction is critical to building trust that will enable the siblings to take more and more authority over time. Our frequent advice to successors: communicate, communicate, communicate.

In some family businesses, the siblings actually buy their parents' ownership. Such a transaction can provide necessary security for the parents as well as give the successors full legal and psychological ownership authority. This approach is particularly relevant if the siblings and business managers see opportunity from aggressive growth, but the senior generation has become more conservative and less eager to try new things. While the founding generation should always be accorded the courtesy of being kept apprised of what is going on at the company, if the siblings are to assume leadership and pursue the important opportunities they want for the business, they may need the ultimate authority for setting strategic direction that comes only with full ownership.

WE CANNOT GET PAST A CONFLICT

Some conflicts in family businesses can appear irrational. These conflicts may have originated years before in a basement brawl or may be due to long-standing resentments, but they can impact business decisions in the present. Emotional or loaded conflicts such as these do not always lend themselves to clear business solutions and can lead to situations where a family feels hopelessly stuck.

In our experience, mediation can help in these situations. A mediator is a neutral third party who works with all relevant stakeholders to find a resolution to the dispute. The mediator helps the parties to communicate and develop a mutually acceptable solution. Compared to other paths for conflict resolution (e.g., lawsuits), mediation is typically faster, less expensive, and more likely to help the family preserve positive relations with one another.

A good mediator facilitates the complicated conversations that may be necessary. He or she helps each individual recognize some of their counterproductive thoughts or behaviors and helps all parties involved to focus on seeking balanced and businesslike solutions. Family business advisors often play this role of mediator very effectively, helping all the stakeholders better appreciate what they have in common and facilitating solution-focused conversations that move the parties to resolve their disagreements.

Occasionally, this process shows a family that their rifts are too severe or the differences too vast to continue as business partners. Awareness of irreconcilable differences can help the family make the hard choices to move forward and not just stay stuck. Previously unthinkable choices, such as the buyout of a family member or the sale of the business, may be deemed necessary. A mediator can help ensure that all stakeholders are appropriately engaged in the process and experience it as fair, and this helps protect the long-term interests of the business and the family, no matter what solution is chosen.

THE "OLD GUARD" RESISTS CHANGES IN LEADERSHIP STYLE AND STRUCTURE

As was indicated in the previous chapter, the transition to the sibling generation typically comes with a number of significant changes in how decisions are made and in business operations. While some non-family executives may embrace these changes, others may passively or actively resist. Some may even seek to subvert change and attempt to split the sibling team by complaining about one sibling to another or to the parents. While it is important to be respectful of valued long-time employees, the siblings must keep their leadership team intact and consistently communicate with all others with a single voice. To that end we suggest siblings develop rules about communication with all stakeholder groups. Typically, the approach is similar to how the siblings handled their parents in the case above. The following are some sample rules from families about stakeholder communication:

> Debate and different views are encouraged among the ownership team behind closed doors. However, once a decision has been made, all owners will support the decision 100 percent in all conversations with other employees.

> If an employee comes to speak to one owner about another owner, the employee will be instructed to speak with the other owner directly.

> One family member is the designated spokesperson for the views of the family and will speak to media and at employee events. This role will be rotated among shareholders annually.

INSIDERS—OUTSIDERS TENSION IN THE SIBLING GENERATION

Sal was in a fury; his brother and sister were not being straight with him about the situation in the business. Just because he didn't work there didn't mean they had a right to keep him in the dark. They kept paying themselves handsome bonuses, yet they were unwilling to increase the dividend this year, and he had to sign off on two line of credit extensions in the past 18 months. Didn't they realize he needed to start budgeting for college tuition for his kids? He was trying to save, but it was difficult just getting by on his teacher's salary. His well-paid siblings just didn't understand that. Sal loved his job and was at peace with his career choice, but he wished his siblings wouldn't treat him like an outsider when it came to matters of the company.

Striking the correct balance between siblings who work in the business and those who work elsewhere can be difficult. Anger and mistrust can develop if some siblings feel they are somehow getting a raw deal. For example, in the case described above, Sal seems to be questioning the salary and bonuses paid to his siblings, hinting that more funds should be available for dividends, in which he would have a share. Of course, working shareholders can also resent their siblings who are not working in the business and feel they are working themselves ragged just to make money for folks who don't appreciate their demanding responsibilities. Regular sibling meetings and open communication as well as ongoing investments in the personal relationships between siblings are the best protection against these issues.

The risk of tension between insiders and outsiders will be exacerbated if siblings are not regularly involved and informed about business matters that concern owners. Note that this is a two-way street. The siblings who are involved with the business need to make sure they keep their other siblings posted, but those who do not work in the business also need to make it their business to stay current and actually read and understand materials about the business or industry that are sent their way. An owner who behaves like a passive shareholder only concerned with economic benefit to his or her pocketbook, will lose credibility as a stakeholder and steward who takes a longer and broader view of the shared enterprise.

Making a habit of strong communication and collaboration between working and non-working shareholders can be challenging if there are lingering feelings in the family that somehow all the shareholders should be working in the business. Some founders may have really hoped that all their children would work in the business and could be disappointed if some of them took other directions. The founder may have provided less ownership education to the inactive shareholders and may act like these shareholders are not very relevant to the business. Some families make a distinction in ownership between siblings who work in the business and those who do not, either restricting ownership to those who work in the business or providing family members not working in the business with fewer or with nonvoting shares. Whatever the choice on how ownership is allocated, all owners should be part of all ownership conversations.

Finally, some managers (family and non-family) may assume shareholders who are not working in the business are totally uninterested and treat them accordingly. Shareholders who do not work in the business should make an extra effort to demonstrate their interest and commitment. Come to important ceremonial functions, spend time getting to know the non-family executives involved in running your company, and ensure they know you value their contributions. Develop your understanding of the company, its strategy, and its results and also express appreciation to your siblings in positions of managerial responsibility for all they do in the business.

"JUNIOR" ISN'T THE BEST-QUALIFIED TO TAKE OVER FOR DAD.

Sometimes things don't go exactly as planned. Mike Jr. came to work for his father's business right out of high school, and he worked hard. He was never great with people or numbers, but he knew how to make the plant run efficiently and was well liked by his crew. Mike's brother Patrick decided to go to college and then worked about ten years in a different city and industry. When he and his wife decided to start a family, Patrick wanted to move back to his hometown so he joined his dad and brother in the family business.

Patrick initially worked in sales, which he had also done at his previous place of employment. He had an immediate impact on the business, opening new markets and growing the business at a pace not seen in 15 years. While he enjoyed sales, he was eager to keep learning and decided to go back to business school at night. He learned important skills in management that he was able to bring to the company. An unintended consequence of all this innovation was some anxiety. Within five years of his arrival, the non-family managers started to worry about what would happen at the time of succession. Who would be put in charge and how would that affect the business and their roles? Most of the executives felt Patrick was the better choice, but some of the guys in the plant were deeply loyal to Mike Jr. who was more like his father in style.

While the norms of inheritance have evolved from straight primogeniture (everything passing on to a firstborn son), the eldest son is still often assumed to be the one to follow in dad's footsteps and succeed him in leadership. If that person is not the best qualified to take over the leadership role, tensions can arise between the siblings, within the family, and even in the business. The best solution to this challenge is to have the siblings determine among themselves how they will select leadership roles and agree to present a united front no matter what the outcome of that process. An active board with independent directors can provide important objectivity regarding the process of leadership selection.

Ideally, the relationships among the siblings are strong enough that they can appreciate each other's strengths and limitations and reach a rational choice. They should all realize that the role of CEO or president is a job requiring certain skills and abilities. Other engaged siblings can contribute in vital ways to their partnership. And remember, it is a sibling team. The successor is not the "new dad," just the leader of a team in which every member is important.

If some employees are concerned about the choice of leaders, the sibling not chosen (most likely Mike in this case) should speak for the ownership team to all the stakeholders about why his brother Patrick is the ideal choice to lead the business into the future.

FOUNDER DIES SUDDENLY AND NO PLANS HAVE BEEN MADE

If a founder dies or becomes disabled unexpectedly and there has been no or little written planning done, stakeholders are left to deal with their feelings of grief and shock while trying to keep the business on track. At the same time, they are confronted with decisions that must be made for the longer term.

One of the best protections against such a crisis is the presence of an established board of directors. A board can offer much needed continuity for the business, which may provide important reassurance to key stakeholders such as suppliers, bankers, and clients. In addition, these business leaders can offer guidance to the surviving spouse and nascent sibling team. We have seen situations where a board member even steps in as an interim CEO for a year or two to allow the business to get its footing before having to confront the choice of a more permanent next leader.

If there is no obvious leader who can step in as an interim president, an alternative is to establish an emergency management team comprised of the active siblings and key non-family executives. Depending on the surviving spouse's comfort and knowledge of the business, she or he should be involved as well as the shares of the founder often pass on to the spouse. The team should meet at least weekly to deal with ongoing business decisions and to consider what leadership decisions and strategic adjustments might best serve in the longer term for the ongoing interests of the business and its owners. Ideally, immediate issues are dealt with by the management team, and the next generation will also be meeting as a group to address the many issues, policies, and guidelines needed for their partnership to succeed in the long term. The guidance offered in this book can provide a good starting point for these important conversations.

Chapter 9

Laying the Foundation for the Cousin Generation to Follow

L ove and strong family ties can blind some families to future risks. When siblings have trusting and close relations with one another, they often resist setting up formal processes and policies because they do not feel they need to create so many structures and systems to manage their company. After all, they grew up together, work well together, share a profound respect for the company and the legacy of their parents, and are simply very busy running the business from day to day. Sibling-owned businesses may occasionally succeed even when they set up only a few formal structures. Yet, even in those cases where harmony has prevailed among siblings, it's a new ball game when the third generation starts to come of age and to enter the business. All of a sudden, parental allegiance may trump filial bonds and even harmonious siblings may find themselves in conflict if they feel their children's future is at stake. As cousins mature, decision-making processes will eventually need to accommodate many more people. Three siblings may perhaps reach joint decisions on the fly, but when there are 17 cousins (who most likely do not all work in the business), new models are essential.

It is beyond the scope of this book to highlight all the challenges and complexities that a business can anticipate for its third generation (See *From Siblings to Cousins: Prospering in the Third Generation and Beyond* in the Family Business Leadership series, which is listed on p. ii). Suffice it to say that just as the founding parents do their children an enormous favor by helping set up the structures and processes that are a foundation for success between siblings, the siblings too must set the stage for their own children's eventual transition into the business. To illustrate the value of this, consider the following two cases:

The Smith brothers from the United Kingdom have worked together all their lives, having transformed a small distribution business started by their father into a wholesale powerhouse. Each of the four contributes in different ways, some more than others, but they love and trust one another and are able to get by with an informal structure of management. Most of their children (six of nine in all) have made careers in the business as well. While many are working hard and all are proud of the family legacy, some are less capable than others.

As the business continues to grow, tensions are starting to show between the cousins due to the lack of oversight or clear policies on basic matters. For example, the four brothers all earn the same salary, though their jobs do not objectively merit the same pay. The brothers have attempted to maintain this notion of parity among their children, but it is causing more harm than good, and the cousins who are the greatest contributors are starting to resent the cousins they feel are not really pulling their weight or are simply less capable. To add insult to injury, those cousins whose mothers are the most vocal seem to get more opportunities for advancement than the others.

In addition, two brothers had three children each, one had two kids, and the youngest only had one. This naturally leads to differences in distribution amounts that come to cousins, but the family has never had any meetings to educate shareholders, so the cousins spent many years being confused and angry. Though today they may understand this is how dividends flow, it still contributes to resentment among cousins.

While most of the cousins indicate they would prefer a more structured HR department and salaries determined by market rates, the brothers (who are still in charge) resist this approach. Some unaddressed sibling rivalry is coming out with a vengeance here, and the "hard-working" brothers fear their "smart brother" may be trying to get better pay for his own kids at the expense of their less accomplished children. The brothers avoid dealing with compensation concerns as they are unwilling to address the discomfort this may create in the family in the short term.

Frustrated by this situation, two of the most competent cousins recently elected to leave the business and work where they can earn a better salary. There is a lot of anger over how this happened, creating new rifts between the brothers and leading some to suspect the departing cousins may be trying to set up a competing business. Whether that happens or not, the cousins who remain in management roles in the family business are in over their heads, a few of the cousins are currently not on speaking terms with each other or with one of the siblings, and all of this is causing the brothers to worry that they may never be able to retire.

By way of contrast, consider the story of Kang Metals, which three brothers, Rick, James, and Larry, inherited from their father. Encouraged by their parents, the three brothers had begun to meet as a sibling team in their early twenties and even started to involve their wives in family meetings twice a year once they started to have children of their own. While the spouses were not involved in ownership decisions, they were kept informed of major events at the company, had an understanding of the roles each of the brothers were playing, and were clear on the shared family values that guided decisions affecting the family and the business.

Through their sibling team meetings, the brothers made a commitment to do what was best for the business. They drafted policies regarding compensation, share ownership, criteria for board membership, and many others. In addition, as none of them felt qualified to manage the overall operations of the business, they hired Florian, a non-family president nearly 15 years ago.

Florian not only helped the brothers to professionalize the company, but he also impressed on them the need to look toward the long-range future of the company and the family. He encouraged them to do estate and succession planning and, despite their initial fears about how they could effectively bring family into the business, to start inviting members of the third generation to join the company.

Today, half a dozen of the Kang cousins, all of whom have experience outside the company, work in the business. Encouraged by their fathers and guided by Florian, they assumed responsibility for building the company *even further. They volunteered to take on the task of succession planning, and recently the cousins elected Larry's daughter, Georgia, as president and CEO of the company and Rick's son, Richard, as executive vice president. What was a small company when the four brothers inherited it has grown significantly under their leadership and is growing still. It now has sales of over $500 million annually and employs more than 900 people. Moreover, the cousins are already consciously preparing for the fourth generation of family leadership and ownership.*

Why has the Kang family been so successful in preserving the business for the family? For one thing, family members placed great value on family harmony and their commitment to each other. The three brothers encouraged all their children to attend family business seminars (whether they had an interest in working in the business or not), where they gained skills and knowledge that they brought back to the business and the family.

The cousins say that Florian served as an excellent mentor. But the real key was the superb example their fathers set for them. "The one thread that wove its way through our thinking was the marvelous relationship that Rick, James, and Larry had as a team," says Georgia. In their meetings, she continues, the cousins often reflect on the spirit of family that their fathers represented to them, and they committed themselves to emulating that spirit.

These two stories—of the Smith brothers and of the Kang family—underscore the critical importance of the sibling generation. What happens at the sibling stage will influence what happens in the business and in the family for a long time to come. Will both family and business be put at risk as they have in the Smith family? Or, as in the Kang family, will the business and family thrive and look forward to yet another generation thanks to the loving team spirit exemplified by siblings in the second generation? While each generation has to set its own goals and develop the systems and structures that support these, the heaviest lifting and most complex change is typically in the transition from the first to the second generation. If the siblings do a good job of establishing strong decision-making and oversight structures, these will likely serve as a stable foundation for many generations to come.

Conclusion: Enjoy the Journey and the Destination

REMEMBER: IT'S A FAMILY

Sometimes with all the time and work required to become an effective and successful ownership and leadership group of siblings, it is easy to lose sight of what a family business is really all about: family. It's about each sibling's own family and extended family, Mom and Dad, brothers and sisters and their spouses, and nieces and nephews. Without their love, happiness, goodwill, and support, a sibling partnership can falter. If things aren't working well for the family, it is fair to ask: why bother?

We hope your sibling team can enjoy the journey as well as savor the results of all the hard work. However, as we have indicated throughout this book, this will not happen by itself or automatically. You need to invest the time to prepare and take time to have fun as a family. Spend time with your spouse and children, of course, but you and your family should also spend time socially with your siblings and their families.

You may feel that you already spend so much time with your siblings at work that you don't want to spend even more time with them away from the business. But this kind of social time serves a special purpose; it enables your spouse and children and their spouses and children to see that all is well among you and your siblings. It also helps them better understand one another so that they will want to support the continuation of the family business. Finally, it is an investment in your personal relationship with your sibling. Like a marriage, a sibling partnership will have its ups and downs, and a reservoir of positive shared experiences will help cushion the inevitable moments of frustration and disagreements you will have in your partnership.

Some ideas for fun: Go on family retreats together. Work together on a family philanthropy project. Go on outings as a group, camping or skiing. Look for ways to have the children—the cousins—spend time together as tots, toddlers, and preschoolers. An important goal is to create good memories for the children as a family because these contribute to having the business continue across generations. When you create an environment in which cousins have a good time together as small children, you're taking some of the first steps to position them for success as the next generation of cousin-owners and leaders of the family business. Also, remember to include siblings who are not working in the business. The focus of these outings is to build family cohesion; they are not business functions.

SUMMARY

Building a successful sibling partnership requires dedication and hard work on the part of parents, spouses, and most especially the siblings themselves.

Parents can help by treating the siblings as a unit, giving them challenging tasks to work on as a team, and resisting the temptation to intervene when things don't go smoothly.

Husbands and wives support the team by educating themselves about the business and about family business in general. They'll find it wise to get to know all the family members directly instead of second-hand through their spouses' views.

If you are in the sibling group, you will enhance your chances for success if you commit yourself to being a unit and take the steps necessary to gain skills in communication, conflict resolution, and shared decision-making. Your chances will be strengthened further if you create an infrastructure of governance, policies, and procedures that provides the framework for effective planning, decision-making and accountability. Such an infrastructure also supports harmony in the team by making decisions less personal and more professional and by encouraging all team members to perform at their highest level and conduct themselves in a mature fashion. The infrastructure includes having a board of directors with respected, independent outsiders and holding a variety of business and family meetings that enhance communication and decision making.

As a sibling team, you will find you have to be vigilant and sensitive to what is going on around you. Be sure that actions by Mom and Dad are not divisive for the group. Take action to make sure all spouses are made to feel part of the sibling partnership, so that you will have their support. Be mindful that all speak with one voice to non-family employees, giving them due respect but not letting them play one of you against the others.

Nurture your personal relationships with one another. Since you have grown and changed over the years, take the time to rediscover one another as adults. Having fun, enjoying one another's company, and finding shared interests outside the business will help you weather rough patches in the business.

And finally, emphasizing your common ground and focusing on a goal larger than yourselves will go a long way toward holding you together as a team and enabling you to deal with your individual differences. Sibling partnerships are an increasingly common phenomenon. As you build your team, keep in mind that the sibling stage presents some of the greatest challenges—and opportunities— that a family business can face. Take heart from the success of other sibling partnerships and pledge yourself to be a positive model for generations of your family yet to come.

References

American Family Business Survey. 2007. *The Mass Mutual, Kennesaw State University, Family Firm Institute American Family Business Survey.* Springfield, MA: MassMutual Financial Group.

Bowen, Murray. 1992. *Family Therapy in Clinical Practice.* Northvale, NJ: Jason Aronson.

Deci, Edward, and Richard Ryan. 1985. *Intrinsic Motivation and Self-Determination in Human Behavior.* New York, NY: Plenum Press.

Elder, G. H., and E. K. Pavalko. 1993. "Work Careers in Men's Later Years: Transitions, trajectories, and Historical Change." *Journal of Gerontology 48* (4): S180– S191.

Gee, S., and J. Baillie. 1999. Happily Ever After? An Exploration of Retirement Expectations." *Educational Gerontology 25:*109–28.

Laird Norton Tyee. 2007. *Family to Family: Laird Norton Tyee Family Business Survey 2007.* Conducted in conjunction with the Austin Family Business Program at Oregon State University and the Albers School of Business and Economics at Seattle University.

Tuckman, Bruce. 1965. "Developmental Sequence in Small Groups." *Psychological Bulletin 63* (6): 384–99.

Ward, J. L. 1987. *Keeping the Family Business Healthy: How to Plan for Continuing Growth, Profitability, and Family Leadership.* San Francisco, CA: Jossey-Bass.

The Authors

Stephanie Brun de Pontet is senior consultant of the Family Business Consulting Group, Inc. and specializes in advising family enterprises facing important transitions. She has extensive experience working with sibling teams, developing training programs to educate next-generation family members, and building the framework for next-generation collaborations. In addition to her consulting work, Stephanie is the executive editor of the *Family Business Advisor* and has coauthored a book, *Building a Successful Family Business Board*, with Drs. Jennifer M. Pendergast and John L. Ward.

Craig E. Aronoff is cofounder, principal, and chairman of the board of the Family Business Consulting Group, Inc., the founder of the Cox Family Enterprise Center, and professor emeritus at Kennesaw State University. He invented and implemented the membership-based, professional service provider-sponsored Family Business Forum that has served as a model of family business education for universities worldwide

Drew S. Mendoza is managing principal of the Family Business Consulting Group, Inc. He was the founding director of the Loyola University Chicago Family Business Center during which time his consulting work addressed family firm succession, family meetings, and developing high functioning sibling and cousin teams. As the managing principal of the Family Business Consulting Group, Drew is currently focused on business development, assessing client needs, and finding the most appropriate resources for clients and prospective clients. In addition to his consulting work, Drew presents on a variety of family business issues for family business centers, trade organizations, and advisor groups.

John L. Ward is cofounder and senior advisor of the Family Business Consulting Group, Inc. He is clinical professor at the Kellogg School of Management. He researches and teaches strategic management, business leadership and family enterprise continuity, governance, and philanthropy.

Index

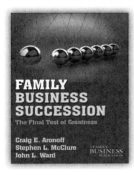

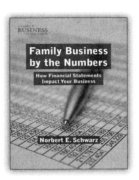